Berlitz

Prague

Original Text Lindsay Bennett
Updater Jeroen van Marle
Cover Photograph Mark Read/Apa
Managing Editor Clare Peel
Series Editor Tony Halliday

POCKET GUIDE

Prague

Fourth Edition (2004)
Updated 2004, 2005, 2006

Photography by:
All photographs are by Pete Bennett/Apa except those on pages 2–3, 11, 14, 18, 24, 26, 30, 34, 36, 40, 49, 52, 53, 55, 65, 82, 88, 91, 94, 99 Glyn Genin/Apa; 20, 22 AKG-images London 3bl; 28 Topham Picturepoint; 2 (centre and bottom), 3 (top right), 18, 32, 79, 81, 83 Phil Wood/Apa; 87 Mark Read/Apa.

CONTACTING THE EDITORS
Every effort has been made to provide accurate information in this publication, but changes are inevitable. The publisher cannot be responsible for any resulting loss, inconvenience or injury. We would appreciate it if readers would call our attention to any errors or outdated information by contacting Berlitz Publishing, PO Box 7910, London SE1 1WE, England. Fax: (44) 20 7403 0290;
e-mail: berlitz@apaguide.co.uk
www.berlitzpublishing.com

The Gothic spires of Our Lady before Týn (page 50) soar high into the Prague sky

Fine frescoes decorate the Loreto (page 38), one of Prague's top places of pilgrimage

The majestic façade of St Vitus Cathedral (page 31) is dazzling

TOP TEN ATTRACTIONS

Charles Bridge (page 45) is a Gothic masterpiece lined with beautiful sculptures

The National Theatre (page 63) is home to the National Opera and Ballet

The rituals of the Astronomical Clock (page 48) celebrate the mystical passing of time

Monuments in the Jewish Quarter (page 53) remember a vanished community

Sternberg Palace (page 28) is home to a fine collection of European Masters

In the Old Royal Palace (page 34), the dimensions of Vladislav Hall seem out of this world

The wide sweep of Wenceslas Square (page 61) brings to mind the Champs-Elysées in Paris

CONTENTS

A ➤ in the text denotes a highly recommended sight

Fact Sheets

INTRODUCTION

Some destinations still have the capacity to give even the most cynical tourist pause for thought, refusing to be reduced to a mere list of museums or galleries. Prague is one such destination – its beauty is truly breathtaking, and its unique character as an important and influential capital city has developed over many centuries.

Set on the banks of the Vltava River (a tributary of the Elbe), the site was chosen both for its strategic advantages and its beauty. The heart of the old city nestles in a bowl formed by rolling hills. Czech folklore tells of a Princess Libuše who had a premonition about a shining city and the exact spot where it should be founded. She married a common ploughman named *Přemysl* to beget the first ruling dynasty, and her descendants were credited with being true and just.

Located in the heart of Europe – perhaps a little further north and west than most people think – Prague (*Praha* in Czech) has been the capital of the ancient realm of Bohemia for centuries. During the Middle Ages it rose to prominence as the capital of Charles IV's vast empire. As Holy Roman Emperor and ruler of much of Western Europe, he was probably the most powerful man in the world at the time (1316–78).

> Legend has it that Princess Libuše, leader of a Slavonic matriarchal tribe, picked the humble peasant Přemysl to be her husband. She bade him go seek a village on the banks of the Vltava and to found a town there, for which she predicted great things. Thus came into being Prague, the 'golden town'.

The Vltava follows its winding course under the bridges of Prague

Charles Bridge and the dark face of Old Town Bridge Tower

In the 16th century the city was a leading centre in the Hapsburg Court and it became the capital of the newly independent country of Czechoslovakia in 1918. During the late 20th century the Czech Republic chafed under the yoke of Communist rule; but when the Iron Curtain fell in 1989, Prague unveiled its hidden wealth of Bohemian treasures and sent out an invitation to the rest of the world.

City of One Hundred Spires

The city presents a unique architectural tapestry, intricately patterned with the legacies of generations. Gothic, Renaissance, Baroque and Art Nouveau gems of exquisite workmanship reveal a rich seam of work by master painters, sculptors and musicians. Also interwoven in the fabric are the threads of political and religious intrigue.

Pride of place must go to Prague Castle, the seat of royal power throughout the Middle Ages. It sits majestically on the top of a low ridge, casting a watchful eye over the events of the city. Royal patronage spawned a court, which in turn drew the rich and powerful. These families spent fortunes building fine mansions and summer palaces, and decorating them with creations by the finest craftsmen of their time. The Church also played its part, but the situation was complicated: Bohemia at this time represented a major battleground between partisans of Catholicism and church reformers. The many impressive cathedrals, churches, chapels, convents and monasteries erected here attest to the vehemence of the struggle – and the eventual triumph of the Catholic Church – and have given Prague the epithet 'city of one hundred spires'.

The dramatic urban landscape alters with every hour. In the mornings, delicate light washes over statuary and domes, while towards sunset rich rays ripen the pastel stucco and gilded spires to give a radiant, golden hue. Passing seasons also introduce a different atmosphere. Although there is no doubt that Prague looks beautiful on a bright summer's day, it is equally enchanting framed by the copper tints of autumn or blanketed by crisp winter snow. Seen at night, it is no less disappointing, with lights bathing a myriad of buildings.

Art, Culture and Leisure

The shimmering reflections on the Vltava River and the waxy glow of thousands of streetlights are two reasons why Prague is considered to be one of the world's most romantic cities. It was this air of romance that inspired Mozart, Beethoven and leading Czech composers Dvořák and Smetana, along with numerous visual artists. Today, it still inspires professional painters and photographers as well as thousands of amateur enthusiasts.

Centuries of the cream of music, theatre and art have nurtured a cultured and urbane society: the people of Prague appreciate their theatres and galleries as much as the visitors do, revelling in the artistic legacy of the Hapsburg years and the flourish of artistic endeavours that accompanied the growing nationalism of the 19th century. Ticket sales for concerts and other performances in the city are deliberately restricted to allow local people from all walks of life to enjoy the unrivalled concert season. However, highbrow pursuits are not the only items on the agenda: the Czech Republic is one of the world's leading beer producers, and locals are just as at home having a few drinks in the city's numerous beer halls or staying out late at a smoky jazz club or rock bar. You can still encounter the angst-ridden café society that gave rise to the writings of Franz Kafka and to the Cubist art of the early part of the 20th century; however, you are much more likely to see people enjoying an ice cream, taking the air in one of the many stretches of parkland or driving around town in the ubiquitous Czech-produced Skoda cars than discussing philosophy.

The Young Generation

Of course, there have been many changes since 1989 for both the city and its people. The younger generation has grown up with the kinds of freedom long taken for granted by teenagers in the West. They throng to the Western bou-

The Romantic Vltava River

As Prague's architecture envelops you in all its stunning glory, you could be forgiven for overlooking one of the city's most beautiful sights: the Vltava itself, its graceful S-shape unwinding in the heart of the city. At times going under the name of Moldau, for centuries it has inspired writers and musicians alike, notably Bedřich Smetana whose symphonic poems dedicated to the river celebrate its lengthy journey across the Czech landscape on its way to Prague.

tiques to buy the latest fashions or pop CDs, and most have mobile phones. However, now that mobiles can be personalised with almost any ring tone the owner desires, the fact that so many young people in Prague opt for the haunting lilts of traditional Slavic melodies is one indication that they have not left their roots behind.

Czech Economy

The Czech economy has been greatly buoyed by the rise in visitor numbers since the Velvet Revolution, a fact that has allowed many historic buildings to benefit from a massive renovation

Bustling Karlova Street

programme that fills some of the city's streets with the smell of paint and damp stucco. You will certainly find it difficult to avoid your fellow travellers, be they honeymooning couples strolling hand in hand along the narrow lanes, students on a budget European 'culture-fest', or large tour groups tramping en masse across the city squares. That Prague manages to satisfy the disparate demands of all these people is a testimony to its diversity. There are few places where you can view a saint's tomb, ponder over the works of several European masters, climb a 14th-century tower, take a carriage ride or river cruise, bargain over the price of fine crystal, go for a romantic stroll or enjoy a classical concerto, all within the space of a few hours. Prague allows you to do this – and more.

A BRIEF HISTORY

Throughout the Christian era Prague's history has been illustrious. The city held a position of power within the mighty Austro-Hungarian dynasty, and figures as distinguished as Good King Wenceslas, the Holy Roman Emperor Charles IV, Jan Hus and the Hapsburg family feature prominently in its story. However, the city has also seen political and religious oppression, intrigue and murder as the machinations of the powermongers were played out, bringing enough sad times to rival the good.

Princess Libuše, mythical founder of the Přemyslids

Located at a natural fording place on the Vltava River, a tributary of the Elbe River, Prague was settled as early as the Stone Age, and remains including tools and jewels have been found in the area. Celtic tribesmen settled here well over 2,000 years ago, followed by a Germanic people. Of more lasting significance, however, was the arrival in the 5th or 6th century AD of the first Slavs, ancestors of the Czechs, who chose to settle on the hilltops for safety.

The second half of the 9th century saw the construction of the castle's original fortifications. It was from here that the Czechs were ruled by the Přemyslid family, a dynasty with mythical roots that extended well into the Middle Ages.

A Saintly Pioneer

Methodius, the Greek preacher, has been credited with bringing Christianity to the Slavs during the late 9th century. He baptised Prince Bořivoj and his wife Ludmilla in around 873. Methodius went on to be declared a true saint, as did Ludmilla, proclaimed patron saint of Bohemia following her assassination.

The grandson of Ludmilla, first of the rulers named Wenceslas (Václav in Czech), held the crown in the 10th century. During his reign a church dedicated to St Vitus was built at Prague Castle. Wenceslas, who was a fervent believer, became the first of the Czech princes to be murdered while carrying out his holy duties – he was ambushed on his way to Mass. It was a family drama of classical proportions, the killer being none other than his younger brother, Boleslav.

Far from being condemned for eliminating the now sainted Wenceslas, Boleslav assumed power and held it for nearly half a century. During his reign, a well-travelled Jewish merchant by the name of Ibrahim ibn Jacob wrote admiringly of Prague as a great and busy trading centre with solid stone buildings. The town became a bishopric in 973, at about the time that the monastery of St George was established on Castle Hill.

In the early 11th century Přemyslid rule was extended to neighbouring Moravia by Břetislav I, the great-grandson of Boleslav. He later became a vassal of the German emperor, paving the way for centuries of German influence. Břetislav's son, Vratislav II, was the first monarch to bear the title of King of Bohemia.

The Wenceslas Dynasty

Prince Wenceslas I, the saint, was not the only Wenceslas I. The second Wenceslas I became king of Bohemia in 1230, and ruled long and well. Encouraging the arts, he presided over a growing prosperity – and population. Since the early 13th century, immigrants from Germany had been moving into Bohemia, and some settled in Prague. In 1257, King Otakar II founded the Lesser Quarter as a German enclave, protected by German law. Under Wenceslas II, Otakar's son, the economy boomed thanks to large finds of silver, and the Prague *groschen* became a stable international currency.

The dynasty's luck eventually ran out with the son of Wenceslas II. In the summer of 1306, early in his reign, the teenage King Wenceslas III went down in history as the last of the Přemyslid kings when he was assassinated in Moravia.

The mosaic of the *Last Judgement* adorns St Vitus Cathedral

Charles the Great

It was yet another Wenceslas who transformed Prague from a provincial town into a global capital. Son of John (Jan) of Luxembourg, who ruled Bohemia for 36 years, he gained a good education in Paris before changing his name to Charles.

Even before his coronation, the future King Charles IV (Karel IV) was deeply involved in the government of Prague and Bohemia. His warm relations with the church led to Prague being promoted to an archbishopric in 1344. Under his direction, centuries of work began on the present St Vitus Cathedral, the resplendent Gothic centrepiece of Hradčany Castle. Early in his reign in 1348, Charles put Prague firmly on the intellectual map of the world by founding Central Europe's first university. He expanded the city to the New Town, thus providing room for artists, craftsmen and merchants from all over Europe. Finally, he gave Prague its Gothic Charles Bridge, still functioning as a beautiful link between the Old Town and the Lesser Quarter 650 years on.

In 1355, Charles acquired yet another royal title when he was crowned Holy Roman Emperor. He ruled nobly over both the empire and Bohemia until his death in 1378.

Religious Strife

The city of Prague should have thrived as the administrative headquarters of the empire that Charles had consolidated, but people and events conspired against it. Charles IV's son and successor, Wenceslas IV, proved an irresolute leader. He turned his back on feuds, revolts and wars and was eventually deposed.

In the most momentous crisis that Wenceslas failed to address, Prague lived through the skirmishes that were preludes to the Reformation. At Bethlehem Chapel, in the Old Town, a priest, theologian and professor named Jan Hus challenged the excesses of the Catholic Church. Hus's

The statue of Jan Hus gazes out over Old Town Square

demands for reform became so vigorous that he was excommunicated, arrested for heresy and finally burnt at the stake in 1415. In the aftermath of his martyrdom his large and loyal following, known as the Hussite Movement, gained momentum, much to the dismay of the papacy. In 1419 a reformist mob invaded Prague's New Town Hall, liberated imprisoned Hussites and threw several Catholic city councillors from the windows. This event, called the First Defenestration of Prague, was to herald a long tradition.

The harried brother of the unfortunate Wenceslas, King Sigismund, marshalled Czech Catholic forces and foreign allies in a crusade against the Hussites. However, the rebels fought back. Their under-equipped, but highly motivated, peasant army won some noteworthy victories, such as at the Battle of Vítkov Hill. The rebels were commanded by a brilliant one-eyed soldier named Jan Žižka, but following his death the leadership foundered, and they were eventually defeated. Their extraordinary saga is still richly recalled in today's Czech Republic.

Sigismund died without leaving a successor. His was followed by the short-lived reigns of his son-in-law Albrecht of Austria, and then of Albrecht's son, Ladislas. A dynamic politician by the name of George of Poděbrady, who was implicated in the death of Ladislas, was elected to succeed him. George aligned himself with the Hussites, to the great displeasure of the neighbouring Catholic kings and the papacy. He was eventually excommunicated and, along with Prague, boycotted by the international diplomatic and business community.

Four Centuries under the Hapsburgs

Absentee kings ruled Bohemia from George's death until 1526, when the Hapsburgs claimed the throne. This zealously Catholic dynasty held sway over what remained of the Holy Roman Empire and focused their attention on protecting their European borders against the very real Muslim threat. By now the Protestant faith had become a powerful influence, in addition to which Bohemia's grave religious divisions were simply another thorn in their side.

In 1576 Emperor Rudolph II came to the throne and remarkably moved his capital from Vienna to Prague. Imperial patronage spurred the arts and sciences to new heights, and splendid Renaissance buildings further embellished the city. Rudolph's principal accomplishment was a decree granting freedom of religion

> **Rudolph II (1583–1611), Prague's emperor under the Renaissance, was fascinated by the occult. He employed a number of alchemists who had access to the castle by means of a network of underground passages.**

to Catholics and Protestants alike. However, the decree was not honoured by Ferdinand II, the Catholic king who succeeded him in 1611, and the inherent religious conflict soon escalated into the misery of the pan-European Thirty Years' War.

The people of Prague witnessed numerous defenestrations *(see page 16)* at the Bohemian Chancellery of Prague Castle. In the rebellion that ensued, Ferdinand was deposed, but his supporters rallied and triumphed at the Battle of the White Mountain in 1620. Restored to power, Ferdinand taught the populace a harsh lesson in loyalty by having two dozen rebel

leaders executed in the Old Town Square and proclaiming Roman Catholicism the only legal religion.

Ferdinand's decisive victory radically changed the now-haggard face of Prague. A large majority of Protestant landowners emigrated, and their property fell into the hands of Ferdinand's supporters. Baroque architecture, in the style favoured in Catholic Italy, came into fashion and the medieval atmosphere of Prague gave way to extravagant 17th-century palaces. New churches signalled the great triumph of the Counter-Reformation. Henceforth, German, not Czech, was spoken in the palace and the courthouse. The tensions arising between Prague's German-speaking and Czech-speaking citizens would persist well into the 20th century.

Counter-Reformation fresco in the Loreto Church cloister

Maria Theresa, daughter, wife and mother of Holy Roman emperors, was the only queen to reign over Prague. Her 16 children included Marie Antoinette, the future queen of France. Under her son and heir, Joseph II, religious tolerance was restored, serfdom abolished and censorship relaxed. On a municipal level, he consolidated the city of Prague from its hitherto separate components: the Castle District (Hradčany), Lesser Quarter, Old Town and New Town. The cultural development of Joseph's Prague can be gauged by its music: in 1787 Mozart was invited to conduct the world premiere of *Don Giovanni* in the Estates Theatre, where it was a huge success.

Industrial Prague

By the middle of the 19th century, Prague's population exceeded 100,000. Factories were built, and a railway to Vienna was opened, marking the start of the Industrial Revolution. Bohemia went on to become the most advanced manufacturing centre of the Austrian Empire.

Another kind of revolution started in 1848, uniting Czech nationalists and the new working class of Prague against the remote, rigid Austrian authorities. The uprising was soon extinguished, but the smouldering nationalist sentiment of the Czechs was not. When Prague's monumental National Theatre opened in 1881, the first work to be performed was a new opera by Smetana, a proud and patriotic saga called *Libuše*. Dvořák too took his inspiration from Czech folk songs. Nationalist Prague was conspicuously out of step with the rhythm of the Hapsburg capital, Vienna, home of the waltz.

The 20th Century

When the heir to the Hapsburg throne, Archduke Franz Ferdinand, was assassinated in June 1914, the Austro-Hungarian Empire was plunged into World War I. From the ashes of a defeated Austria-Hungary, an independent Czechoslovakian republic was proclaimed in October 1918, comprising Bohemia, Moravia and Slovakia. The first president of the First Republic was Tomáš G. Masaryk, an admired professor of philosophy, who was re-elected three times before his death in 1937.

Czechoslovakia was at the eye of the storm that whipped itself up into World War II. In 1938 Hitler demanded self-determination for Czechoslovakia's German-speaking citizens. In order to appease him, Britain and France handed over the country's western provinces. Hitler then threatened to rain

The Prague Spring was brutally crushed by the Soviet tanks

bombs on Prague unless the remainder of the country was made a German protectorate. The government of what remained of Czechoslovakia's Second Republic capitulated. Six long years of occupation were to follow before Soviet troops liberated the city in May 1945.

At the parliamentary elections of 1946, the communists won nearly 40 percent of the votes. The non-communist pre-war president Edvard Beneš, elected again, invited the veteran communist leader Klement Gottwald to form a coalition cabinet.

Gottwald, who had spent the war years in the Soviet Union, seized his big chance in 1948. When several non-communist ministers resigned in protest of his one-sided policies, Gottwald packed the government with supporters. Non-communist Foreign Minister Jan Masaryk, son of Tomáš, was found dead below his office window at the foreign ministry – victim of another defenestration.

Gottwald, as the new president, framed a five-year economic plan, cracked down on the churches and purged his opponents outside and inside the party; scores were executed and thousands arrested. The show trials went on under Antonín Novotný, while farmers were forced into collectives and the arts were smothered under Socialist Realism.

A reform movement in the late 1960s culminated in the 'Prague Spring' under Alexander Dubček, the head of the Slovak communist party. Unshackling the press and the arts, Dubček promised 'socialism with a human face'. But this was 20 years too early. On 21 August 1968, reform was crushed by the armed forces of the Soviet Union – ostensibly there by invitation and aided by Poland, Bulgaria, East Germany and Hungary. As the rest of the world watched massive tanks rumbling through Wenceslas Square, Prague wept. The new party chiefs returned to hard-line traditions even when the winds of change finally blew in from Moscow in the form of *perestroika*.

New Challenges

In 1989 the 'Velvet Revolution' once again saw Wenceslas Square as the backdrop to repression *(see box below)*. A rehabilitated Dubček was elected chairman of a rejuvenated parliament. Havel, freshly out of jail for dissident activities, was proclaimed president. In June 1992 Václav Klaus became prime minister, with Havel renouncing his position as federal

The Velvet Revolution

On 17 November 1989, an event took place that should have been a peaceful student demonstration but turned into a mass movement that police attempted to quell by clubbing protesters. Thousands had gathered on Wenceslas Square to call for the introduction of democracy, waving their house keys as a symbol of protest against 40 years of communism. The next day, the regime stepped down in what would become known as Eastern Europe's quietest revolution. Although numerous communist figures have continued to wield power from the wings under the presidency of former playwright Václav Havel, the country has nonetheless made remarkable progress, most notably in the economic field.

president. However, old tensions between Czechs (including Moravians and Silesians) and Slovaks resurfaced, threatening a violent split within the country. Politicians dealt swiftly with the problem by talking rather than fighting. On 1 January 1993 Czechoslovakia was peaceably divided into the Czech and Slovak republics, and in February Havel was returned to power as president of the new Czech Republic, with its capital in Prague.

Since the Czech Republic became its own country, it has strived to become more Westernised and technologically modern, in 2002 becoming the first former Soviet satellite state to host a NATO summit. But challenges have abounded. The summer of 2002 brought devastating floods, caused by rainstorms which paralysed much of Prague's metro system for months. The Czechs recovered, only to be faced with the problem of replacing their beloved Havel, now in ill health. Klaus eventually succeeded him early in 2003, after two rounds of unsuccessful elections.

In June 2003 the country voted overwhelmingly to join the EU. Drastic economic and regulatory reforms have since been implemented, and Prague's increasingly vibrant cultural scene is just one testimony to this. In 2004 the Republic joined the EU proper, and since then has witnessed the resignation of two prime ministers. Jiri Paroubek took over the Social Democratic coalition in April 2005. It is hoped that the country's newfound economic prosperity, combined with the elite status of being a member of the EU, will further usher the country into a new era of influence.

Former president Václav Havel

Historical Landmarks

*c.*400BC Invasion by a Celtic tribe, the Boii, who give Bohemia its name.

AD 400 Arrival of the Slavs.

900–1306 Rule of the Přemyslid dynasty; building of Prague Castle.

935 Murder of Prince Wenceslas, patron saint of Bohemia, by his brother and successor Boleslav.

1306 Assassination of the young King Wenceslas II and end of the Přemyslid dynasty.

1344 Prague becomes an archbishopric.

1348–78 Reign of Charles IV; building of Charles Bridge.

1398–1415 Jan Hus preaches religious reform and is burnt at the stake.

1420–1526 Hussite Wars. George of Poděbrady crowned king in 1458.

1576 Prague becomes capital of the Hapsburg Empire.

1609 Decree granting religious freedom.

1618 Decree revoked by Ferdinand II. Thirty Years' War ensues.

1620 Catholic victory at Battle of the White Mountain. Repressive measures against Protestants resulting in large-scale exile.

1740–1945 Bohemia becomes part of the Austro-Hungarian Empire.

1848 Nationalist revolution in Prague.

1918 Independent Republic of Czechoslovakia proclaimed.

1938 Munich Agreement cedes the Sudetenland to Hitler.

1939–45 Nazi invasion and occupation.

1945 Prague liberated by the Resistance and the Red Army.

1948 Czechoslovakia becomes a people's republic.

1968 Prague Spring.

1989 Velvet Revolution. Havel elected president of Czechoslovakia.

1992 Slovakia gains independence.

1993 Havel elected president of the Czech Republic.

2003 President Václav Havel steps down; succeeded by Václav Klaus.

2004 The Czech Republic joins the EU.

2005 After a political crisis, Jiri Paroubek becomes Prime Minister.

2006 The new flood defence system is tested as the river rises to high levels during the spring melt.

WHERE TO GO

Prague is probably one of the most appealing cities to visit in the world. Almost every corner reveals an architectural treasure dating from the 13th century to the present day, and numerous fine, large mansions house impressive art collections, folk artefacts or musical masterpieces. You can walk across the heart of the city in one hour along a grid of traffic-free streets, although there is an inexpensive and unobtrusive public-transport system for those wanting a more leisurely option. Several tracts of land on the outskirts have been left green, and there you can sit and enjoy the sunshine and birdsong.

This guide divides Prague into its traditional smaller settlements of Hradčany (the Castle District), the Lesser Quarter (Malá Strana), the Old Town (Staré Město) and the New Town (Nové Město). The major historical and architectural attractions of each are highlighted in turn, not forgetting Prague's famous bridge, the Charles Bridge, linking the city across the Vltava River. The city's suburbs also contain sights worthy of a visit and are only a short metro or tram ride away. Finally, a selection of day trips from the city – either independently or with an organised tour – provides ideas for those wishing to explore the surrounding country.

HRADČANY (THE CASTLE DISTRICT)

On catching your first sight of Prague Castle from across the Vltava River you will be taken aback by its vast size. Not for the Hapsburgs a simple stone stronghold: rather, a citadel equal in area to that of a small town, its numerous fine buildings an imposing reminder of the power of royalty through the centuries. From its beginnings some 1,000 years ago, it developed

The figures on the Astronomical Clock perform their hourly rituals

to perform important ceremonial functions in addition to its protective ones. In the present day, part of the castle has been renovated to house the office of the president of the Czech Republic, consolidating its leading role in diplomatic circles.

The site for the castle was originally picked because of its ridge-top position, which affords excellent views of the town and river valley below. Today's visitors are faced with a choice of three entrances, of which the ceremonial gate at the west side is the starting point of most guided tours. It is also the highest point of the entire castle complex. From here you will be walking downhill towards the steps on the east side.

Hradčany Square

Before entering the castle take a look around **Hradčany Square** (Hradčanské náměstí), which forms an irregular open space outside the gates. Several important grand residences

The changing of the guard at Prague Castle

were built here in close prox-
imity to the seat of power,
most of which underwent a
comprehensive process of
restoration during the 1990s.
In a small grassy area at the
centre of the square stands a
plague column, erected by
grateful survivors after an
outbreak of the disease in the
18th century.

Prague's treasures in-
clude its wealth of green
open spaces, from the
Renaissance royal gar-
dens north of the castle
to the Hradčany garden
in the south, and the
Waldstein Palace gar-
den, with its handsome
sculptures and statues.

On the west side of the square are the **Tuscan Palace**
(Toskánsky palác), a late 17th-century Baroque residence
thought to have been designed by French architect Jean-
Baptiste Mathey, and its neighbour, the former **Martinic
Palace** (Martinický palác), in earlier Renaissance style. The
Tuscan Palace now hosts concerts in its main hall and inner
courtyard, where renovations revealed *sgraffito* (patterns
incised on a flat wall of plaster to create a three-dimensional
effect of shade and depth) depicting biblical scenes.

Across the park, **Schwarzenberg Palace** (Schwarzenber-
ský palác) is perhaps the most distinctive building on the
square. Each façade is covered with brick-like *sgraffito*, its
purpose being to link the disparate architectural styles of the
palace into a coherent whole. The palace was built for the
Lobkowicz family by the Italian architect Agostini Galli in
the mid-1500s, which lent it far more of a Florentine influence than other buildings of the time. The palace is currently
undergoing extensive restoration, in preparation for housing
the National Gallery's collection of Old Masters in 2007.

The most ornate building on the square is the **Archbishop's
Palace** (Arcibiskupský palác) sitting just next to the castle
entrance. The house became the Archbishop's Palace after
the Counter-Reformation in 1562 and its position was an

The Feast of the Rose Garlands, by Dürer, in the National Gallery

indication of the power of the Catholic Church and its influence on the Hapsburg monarchy. The façade was redesigned in the 1760s in high-rococo style. It is only open to the public on one day each year, Maundy Thursday (the Thursday before Easter).

Next door to the palace is one of the major art galleries of Prague, despite a less-than-enticing entranceway. A cobbled alleyway leads to **Sternberg Palace** (Šternberský palác, Hradčanské náměstí 15; open Tues–Sun 10am–6pm; admission charge), home of Franz Sternberg who was a great patron of the arts during the late 18th century. The handsome Baroque building now houses the Czech Republic's **National Gallery of European Art** (Národní galerie). Its fine body of old masters dating from the 14th to the 18th century serves as a reminder that the Hapsburg dynasty was the most powerful of its time, ruling over the Austro-Hungarian Empire of which Prague was a leading light. Their collection incorporates work by the finest artists of their respective eras. Flemish and Dutch art features particularly strongly with works by the Brueghel dynasty, along with Peter Paul Rubens, Rembrandt and Frans Hals. Italian artists are represented by a wealth of 14th- and 15th-century decorative pieces from churches in Tuscany. Among the later paintings, works by Tintoretto and El Greco stand out. Perhaps the most noted painting in the collection is to be found in the Austrian and German section. Along with works by Hans Holbein and his son hangs the *Feast of the Rose Garlands* by Albrecht Dürer, with two Hapsburg family members depicted on the canvas.

After visiting the gallery you may want to take a short break before exploring the castle proper. Just to the south of the castle gate a spot with a panoramic view over the city allows you to catch your breath and capture a few wonderful images on film. There is also a café serving refreshments.

Prague Castle

Building work on the **castle** was begun in the 9th century. By the beginning of the 14th century it housed the palace, churches and a monastery. Refurbished during the reign of Charles IV, it was ravaged by fire in 1541 and most of the buildings were reconstructed in the Renaissance style, fashionable at the time. This gave rise to the unified appearance of many of the buildings within the precinct walls. The castle eventually became a backwater when the Austro-Hungarian Empire chose Vienna as its permanent base, but it was thoroughly renovated in the early 1920s just after Czech-

Legend has it that the ghost of a large black dog haunts the Hradčanské náměstí entrance to Prague Castle. Between 11pm and midnight it appears, and far from being aggressive accompanies passers-by as far as the Loreto before vanishing into thin air.

oslovakia became independent. Surrounding the walls are many gardens offering a peaceful retreat from the sometimes crowded rooms and galleries within.

Enter the castle proper through the ornate gates crowned with heroic statues of fighting giants. Sombre, uniformed guardsmen maintain a silent sentry as you pass through. From this first courtyard – added in the 18th century – **Matthias Gate** (Matyášova brána), the entranceway dating from 1614 that once formed a triumphal arch over moats (now filled in), leads to the second courtyard. Immediately ahead is the entrance to the **Holy Cross Chapel** (kaple svatého Kříž), built by Anslemo Lurago in 1753.

The Golden Portal, once the main entrance to the cathedral

Housed on the north side of this courtyard, in what were once the castle stables, is the **Picture Gallery of Prague Castle** (Obrazárna Pražského hradu). The gallery displays works mainly collected by Rudolf II during his reign (1583–1612). Much of the collection of this passionate man of the arts was taken to Vienna in the years after his reign or lost to the Swedish forces who took it as booty in 1648. Still, the gallery boasts some superb works by Tintoretto, Veronese and Rubens. Here visitors can also enter the north gardens through an archway.

St Vitus Cathedral

A narrow passage leads to the third courtyard of the castle and a sudden view of the immense and awe-inspiring façade of **St Vitus Cathedral** (katedrála svatého Víta; open daily 9am–5pm; admission charge to crypt and chancel), looming up just a few steps away. The towers and spires dwarf the surrounding buildings, at first glance altering one's perception of scale. The cathedral acts as a reliquary for numerous national treasures and the bones of some of the Czech Republic's most famous and revered individuals. The first church on this hallowed ground was built in the 10th century by Prince Wenceslas, who was interred in the rotunda after his premature death. The present edifice was begun in 1344 on the occasion of Prague being declared a bishopric. Charles IV decided that the new

> Of particular note over the triple-arched arcade of the Golden Portal is the mosaic of the *Last Judgement*, created by Venetian artists in 1370. It is composed of glass, pieces of quartz and other natural stones, as well as sheets of gold leaf slipped between two stones for a gilded effect. The Virgin Mary, John the Baptist, the Apostles, Charles IV and his wife Elizabeth de Poméranie are all represented, not forgetting the six patron saints of Bohemia.

cathedral should be in the style of the great religious buildings of France and invited Matthias of Arras to design and build it. After Matthias's death, the work was continued by Peter Parler, a German architect, himself followed by his two sons. Work was disrupted during the Hussite uprisings and was intermittent through the following centuries, in fact the whole building was not regarded as complete until 1929. The main entrance is now through the west doorway, but until the 19th century it was the south door – or Golden Portal – that provided entry. The porch of the latter doorway is highly decorated

Stained-glass window by Mucha in the cathedral (detail)

and crowned with an ornate mosaic of the *Last Judgement (see box on previous page)*. To the left, a Gothic window is filled with delicate gold filigree work.

Once visitors have entered the cathedral, its gigantic proportions are immediately apparent. There are over 18 separate chapels lining the walls. The 19th- and 20th-century element of the cathedral (near the main entrance) contains a chapel with stained glass by Alphonse Mucha, greatly admired for his Art Nouveau artwork. However, the eye is automatically drawn down the core of the building to the magnificent chancel built by Parler in the 1370s. The towering vaults, decorated with delicate tracery, are a high point in Gothic architectural achievement. These are underpinned by elaborate stained-glass windows.

Several of the chapels in this area of the cathedral deserve further examination but none more so than **Wenceslas Chapel** (kaple svatého Václava), dedicated to Saint Wenceslas or the Good King Wenceslas of the Christmas carol as he is more commonly known. Parler created a wonderful Gothic room to house the tomb of the prince, on the same spot as it had been in the previous Romanesque rotunda. The walls are decorated with precious stones and gold leaf interspersed with several ornate frescoes illustrating scenes from the life of the saint. Behind the chapel is a small room containing the coronation jewels. Seven separate keys are needed to unlock the door to the chamber and the jewels remain out of view except for on certain state occasions.

Next to the Wenceslas Chapel are stairs leading to the **crypt** where you can see the walls of earlier religious structures. This room holds the remains of Charles IV and members of his family, along with the tomb of Rudolf II. Above the crypt, in the main level of the cathedral, several other noteworthy rulers are interred: Ferdinand I lies in a large white marble tomb with his wife, and son Maximilian; and an ornate silver tomb holds the remains of Jan of Nepomuk, who was thrown from Charles Bridge in 1393 and declared a saint in the early days of the Counter-Reformation.

To the north of the cathedral you will find **Mihulka Powder Tower** (Prašna věž), part of the 15th-century defensive walls and later used as a foundry and gunpowder workshop. Rumours abounded that experiments in alchemy were being conducted here, and a modern museum delves into these mysterious activites and also documents the tower's official function.

Powder Tower sits beneath the great spires of the cathedral

The Royal Palace

The third courtyard of the castle opens out to the east of the cathedral. Walk past the old chapterhouse where you will find a heroic statue of St George. The south side of the courtyard is dominated by the **Old Royal Palace** (Starý královský palác; open daily 9am–5pm; admission charge), home to Bohemian rulers from the 11th century till the Hapsburg takeover. Its somewhat modest façade conceals a fascinating building whose architectural style spans several centuries. The Romanesque early palace forms the foundations of the present structure, built during the last years of Přemyslid rule. Charles IV later enlarged the palace but it was Vladislav Jagiello in the late 1400s who created the opulent throne chamber. When it was completed in 1502, **Vladislav Hall** (Vladislavský sál) was the largest unsupported secular hall in the world and today its wide expanse and roof supported by ribbed vaults is one of Prague's highlights.

Vladislav Hall

In the 17th century the hall was used as a meeting place, but in earlier times royal tournaments were held there with competitions in horsemanship. The horses were ridden up a wide, gently sloping staircase to the hall, which is now used by the many groups who tour the palace. Serious business went on in the two rooms leading off Vladislav Hall. The **Bohemian Chancellery** (Česká kancelář) was used for Bohemian government business, and it was from this room that two governors and their clerks were defenestrated in 1618, precipitating the Thirty Years' War. **Diet Hall** (Stará sněmovna) was the medieval parliament room. It was badly damaged in the fire of 1541 and rebuilt in the style of the time.

The Old Royal Palace also houses the **Story of Prague** exhibition (open daily 9am–5pm; admission charge), which uses castle models, films and artefacts to tell the history of Prague Castle.

St George's Basilica

St George's Basilica

From the Royal Palace, walk east to another open square – St George's (náměstí U svatého Jiří). Here the buildings flaunt an ochre stucco façade. On the corner is the entrance to **St George's Basilica** (Bazilika svátého Jiří; open Tues–Sun 10am–5pm; admission charge), founded in the early 9th century and said to be the oldest surviving church in Prague. The interior is austere in true Romanesque style, although it has been extensively restored over the centuries, with the scant remains of original ceiling frescoes. The basilica is the resting place of Queen Ludmilla, patron saint of Bohemia, and other members of the Přemyslid dynasty. Towards the end of the 9th century the **Convent of St George** (klášter svatého Jiří; open Tues–Sun 10am–5pm; admission charge) was established next to the basilica. The religious sanctuary was rebuilt many times over the centuries before finally being dissolved in 1782. Today it houses the National Gallery's collection of **Baroque and Mannerist Art** (Tues–Sun 10am–5pm). Among the notable works by Bohemian painters on display are the *Bust of the Talking Apostle* painted in 1725

by Petr Brandl (1668–1735), and *Self Portrait* (1711) by Jan
Kupecký (1667–1740), which shows the artist working on a
portrait of his wife. There are also two delightful landscapes
by Roland Savery (1576–1639).

The Eastern Sector of the Castle

From the convent it is only a short walk to the eastern sector
of the castle. **Golden Lane** (Zlatá ulička) nestles against the
northern ramparts of the castle, lined with a wonderful array
of old cottages dating from the 16th century. They were first
occupied by archers conscripted to defend the castle and later
by craftsmen – goldsmiths included, to whom the street owes
its name. Some said that the street was even a dwelling place
for alchemists. By the beginning of the 20th century, it was an
enclave for the poor. The writer Franz Kafka lived here in
1916 with his sister. Today the cottages have been restored to

The colourful 16th-century cottages of Golden Lane

picture perfection and again house the products of craftsmen and pretty souvenir shops. Just watch your head as you enter, as the lintels are extremely low.

Three attractions fill the route from Golden Lane to the east gate. **Lobkowicz Palace** (Lobkovický palác), built in the aftermath of the 1541 fire, currently houses the **Národní Museum** of the history of Bohemia up to the revolution of 1848 (open Tues–Sun 9am–5pm). The building also houses temporary exhibitions and is occasionally used as a concert hall. Across the street are the **Black Tower** (Černá věž), whose origins reach back to the 12th century, and **Dalibor Tower** (Daliborka), which was used as a prison and named after its first prisoner, a young knight whose plight was also the inspiration for an opera by Czech composer Bedřich Smetana.

The Singing Fountain, decorated with flowers, animals, Greek gods and a set of bagpipes, is by the Italian sculptor Francesco Terzio. Restoration work has unfortunately meant that the hollow metal of the basin no longer produces music.

The steps below this last tower lead down to the Malostranská metro station and the city. In summer they play host to souvenir sellers who sit beneath colourful sunshades. A lookout offers panoramic views and there is access to the gardens below the Royal Palace – resplendent after recent renovations.

The area of Hradčany, although dominated by the castle, offers other attractions to explore. To the north of the fortifications themselves and across from the deep moat – now a forested depression – stands the **Belvedere Palace** (Belvedér palác), built in the 16th century by Ferdinand I and considered to be the only pure Italian Renaissance building north of the Alps. It was used as a summerhouse, and the surrounding **Royal Gardens** must have been a welcome area of relaxation

The 18th-century Loreto

for court members. They would have been greatly amused by the **Singing Fountain**, erected in 1568, whose bronze bowls would resonate when hit by the jets of water *(see box on previous page)*. Unfortunately, much of the rich sculpture work that originally decorated the garden was plundered by Swedish forces in 1648, but it makes a pleasant place to relax for today's visitors.

The Loreto

Walking west, away from the castle entrance on Hradčany Square, you will arrive at another open square, Loretánské náměstí. Here you will find the beautifully ornate Baroque façade of the **Loreto** (Loreta; open Tues–Sun 9.15am–12.15pm and 1–4.30pm; admission charge), one of Bohemia's most important centres of Christian pilgrimage. Its origins date back to the Counter-Reformation of the 1620s when, in order to increase faith in the Catholic religion, the Hapsburgs built replicas of the sacred Santa Casa of Loreto in Italy all across their land. It was said that this original Santa Casa (Holy House and home of the Virgin Mary) had been carried by holy men – or transported by angels – from Nazareth when Islam had overrun the Holy Land at the turn of the first millennium. However, Prague's **Santa Casa** soon developed into far more than a simple shrine. By 1661 it was surrounded by handsome cloisters, to be followed by Baroque decoration and a distinctive belltower created by Christoph and Kilian Ignaz Dientzenhofer (father and son), two of the most skilled architects of their time. Gifts poured in from around the kingdom, and the treasury of the Loreto displays its amazing wealth, including a gold-plated and diamond-encrusted monstrance dating from 1699.

Across the square from the Loreto is the expansive façade of **Černín Palace** (Černínský palác), which occupies the entire west flank. Built for the Černíns, an influential diplomatic family in the 17th century, the palace was huge, measuring an astounding 150m (500ft) in length. Its size was even said to have displeased Leopold I who felt that it rivalled the Royal Palace in splendour. Today it houses the Czech Foreign Ministry, and it was from one of these windows that Jan Masaryk was pushed to his death in 1948 as the communists rose to power.

North of the square lies what is perhaps the prettiest, most unspoiled district in Prague. **Nový Svět** was formerly the poorest quarter in the castle district and as such was left undeveloped. Today it is home to many artists and has not yet been invaded by tourist shops or ticket sellers.

A Priceless Library

The Strahov Monastery *(see next page)* holds some 130,000 volumes, of which 3,000 are manuscripts (the oldest one is the *Strahov Gospel*) and 2,000 first editions. The library also has the distinction of housing the manuscript of the *Gerlaci Chronicon* (1220) and the first edition of the work by Nicholas Copernicus, *De Revolutionibus Orbium Cœlestium* ('On the Revolution of the Celestial Orbs'), in which the famous astronomer explains that it is the earth that revolves around the sun and not vice versa.

Strahov Monastery

Situated a couple of minutes west of Loreto Square and overlooking the river and city is **Strahov Monastery** (Strahovský klášter; open daily 9am–noon and 1pm–5pm; last admission 30 minutes before closing; admission charge), founded in 1140. The complex was situated outside the protection of the city at the end of the road linking Bohemia to what is now Germany, and it was the first such building for the Premonstratensian order. By devoting itself to research it continued to function until 1952 when it was dissolved by the communist regime and the complex taken over for museums. Little remains of the original Romanesque buildings save traces of Gothic and Renaissance features. The monastery is now almost wholly Baroque in style, including two distinctive white towers.

The monastery houses the magnificent **Theological and Philosophical Libraries**, which were built in 1672 and the late 1700s respectively, and can be viewed from the doorway. The walls are a sight to behold, with bookcase upon bookcase of polished timber filled with numerous valuable editions, all aged parchment bound in leather. The eye is drawn up the cases to the highly decorated frescoed ceilings. The 18th-century cabinet of curiosities in the connecting hall houses a stuffed dodo. One religious building remains, the **Church of Our Lady** (kostel Panny Marie), with its rococo gilding and ceiling paintings of cherubs. Mozart is said to have played the organ in the church in 1787.

Ecclesiastical symbols at Strahov Monastery

MALÁ STRANA

Lying below the castle and reaching across to the banks of the Vtlava River is **Malá Strana**, the Lesser Quarter or Little Quarter. The area was first settled in the 13th century when Otakar II invited German craftsmen to settle in Prague. Several fierce fires destroyed the early town, so although the street plan remains faithful to Otakar's original instructions, the majority of the buildings date from a later period. Following the Counter-Reformation in the mid-17th century, Malá Strana became fashionable with wealthy Hapsburgs, and their money was invested in

The Church of St Nicholas

large mansions replete with Renaissance and Baroque details. Malá Strana is still a residential area, a factor which gives it an intimate atmosphere tangibly different to that of Staré Město just across the river *(see page 47)*.

Lesser Quarter Square

The heart of this quarter is **Lesser Quarter Square** (Malostranské náměstí) but its fine mansions, whose arcades straddle the cobbled pavements, have been somewhat overshadowed by the busy tram intersection here. In the centre of the square sits the **Church of St Nicholas** (kostel svatého Mikuláše; open daily 9am–4.30pm; admission charge), one of the most prominent buildings on the Prague skyline and

Emblem of the House at the Three Fiddles, on Nerudova

on the Prague skyline and one of the architectural highlights of the city. The building is perhaps the crowning glory of the Dientzenhofer dynasty and was completed just after the death of Kilian. Work began in the first years of the 18th century but the church was not finished until 1755. The distinctive 75-m (245-ft) dome dominates the surrounding buildings. The interior of the church is considered a Baroque masterpiece, with ceiling frescoes by the Viennese artist Johann Lukas Kracker featuring scenes from the life of St Nicholas, and Franz Palko's *Celebration of the Holy Trinity* gracing the inside of the dome. The two statues below that of St Nicholas above the altar are of St Ignatius Loyola and St Francis Xavier. The church organ has 2,500 pipes and 44 registers, and was once played by Mozart.

To the north of the square is the street of Letenská where you will see the **Church of St Thomas** (kostel svatého Tomáše) abutting the road. Originally founded in 1257, it was one church that remained Catholic throughout the Hussite uprising, and at the onset of the Counter-Revolution became a major focus of Catholic worship. In 1723 the church was badly damaged during a storm, and Kilian Ignaz Dientzenhofer was commissioned to oversee its rebuilding. St Thomas was once the church of a large monastery that had the sole right to brew beer within Prague; the brewery closed as recently as 1951, but the medieval building is still used as the beer hall called At St Thomas's (U svatého Tomáše) where you can enjoy a rather touristy version of traditional Czech hospitality.

As you walk towards the Malostranská metro station you will pass the high walls of **Waldstein Palace** (Valdštejnský palác). This extensive complex was the first Baroque palace in Prague and was built for Albrecht von Wallenstein, a favourite military commander of Ferdinand II. He began work on the palace in 1624 but soon fell victim to his own publicity: he was killed on the king's orders in 1634 when he was discovered to be holding secret talks with the enemy. The palace is now used for concerts and state occasions but you can enter the gardens for free and enjoy the formal lawns, fountains and statuary. In the building are housed copies of works by the celebrated sculptor Adriaen de Vries – the originals having been stolen by Swedish forces during the Thirty Years' War.

West of Lesser Quarter Square is **Nerudova**, named after poet Jan Neruda, who once lived here. There are a number of fine buildings on this road, each distinguished by an emblem as they were built before the introduction of street numbers. Look out for 'The Three Fiddles' at No. 12 or 'The Green Lobster' at No. 43. Thun-Hohenstein Palace at No. 20, its ornate entranceway framed by huge eagles, is now the Italian Embassy; the Morzin Palace at No. 5 now serves as a diplomatic base for Romania.

South of Lesser Quarter Square, the houses are a little

Church of Our Lady in Chains

less grand but the streets are refreshingly peaceful and devoid of tourist shops. Walk down Karmelitská to find the **Church of Our Lady of Victories** (kostel Panny Marie Vítězná) on your right, named in honour of the victory at the Battle of White Mountain in 1620. Most visitors come to see the Holy Infant of Prague – a wax effigy brought from Spain in 1628 and said to be able to work miracles.

From the church, cross the street and head east to **Maltese Square** (Maltézské náměstí), filled with Baroque palaces, many of which are now embassy buildings. The square is named after the knights of Malta who were granted the nearby 12th-century **Church of Our Lady in Chains** (kostel Panny

Kampa Island watermill

Marie pod řetězem) as a gift from King Vlasislav. Here they built a large priory that provided protection for the Judith Bridge across the Vltava. The church's odd name refers to the chain used to close the monastery gates. The church and surrounding priory buildings reveal vestiges of every era, from the Gothic to the Baroque.

Kampa Island and Petřín Hill

Located nearby, Grand Priory Square (Velkopřevorské náměstí) leads across a bridge to tiny **Kampa Island**. Here you will find the fading mural of John Lennon – now surrounded by graffiti. This painting acted as a focus for youth unrest in the final days of Communist rule. The branch of the river separating Kampa Island from the Lesser Quarter is only 3m (10ft) wide and was used to power watermills in days gone by. The island now boasts a pretty cobbled square and a large park.

A street artist on Charles Bridge

Go down Karmelitská and, as it becomes Újezd, you will see the green parkland of **Petřín Hill** to your right. The vast, open area stretching all across the hillside is in fact four different parks, but no one quibbles over the name. You can walk up the hill towards **Petřín Lookout** (Petřínská rozhledna) at the summit, but it is far less taxing to take the funicular running constantly throughout the day and evening. Once at the top you can stroll along the relatively level footpaths to explore the park's attractions. These include the **Observation Tower** – a mini Eiffel Tower – built for the Prague Industrial Exhibition in 1891, a children's playground, three churches and the remnants of the **Hunger Wall** (Hladová zed') – a city wall built by Charles IV and said to have been a community project that would have provided work, and therefore food, for the poor.

Charles Bridge

East of Lesser Quarter Square is Mostecká (Bridge Street). This short, shop-lined thoroughfare leads to the river and to one of the highlights of a visit to Prague: **Charles Bridge** (Karlův most).

Probably one of the most famous bridges in the world, the 520m- (1,700ft-) long Charles Bridge was built across the Vltava in the mid-14th century following the destruction of the previous Judith Bridge in a flood. Charles IV and his architect, Peter Parler, were determined to build a bridge that would last. But even they could not have imagined that it would last 600 years and counting.

The original bridge was a very functional structure with little embellishment. At the Malá Strana end there were two towers: **Judith Tower** (dated *c.*1190), the smaller of the two, survives as the only reminder of the Judith Bridge. Lesser Quarter Bridge Tower was built as a gateway to the town. Today it is open to the public and offers majestic city views. At the Old Town end of the bridge is **Old Town Bridge Tower**, a masterpiece of Gothic architecture with a fine interior viewing room. This is also open to the public.

Charles Bridge at dusk, with Prague Castle in the background

The numerous statues that now make the bridge unmistakeable were mainly added in the early 18th century when the Italian fashion for bridge decoration spread throughout Europe. The exception to this is the statue of **St John Nepomuk** (Jana Nepomuckého), which was erected in 1683 following his violent demise at the hands of King Wenceslas IV and long before the saint was canonised. When his lifeless body was thrown from the bridge onlookers claimed that a holy spirit was seen rising from it, and the story heightened his revered status. The bronze relief below Nepomuk's statue, the one with five stars on the halo around the head, depicts the final moment of the saint; it's polished each day by the hands of thousands of tourists who hope it brings good luck.

The bridge carried traffic until the 1950s – in fact, until the mid-19th century it was the only way to cross the river – but it is now reserved for pedestrians only. During the day Charles Bridge can be one of the busiest parts of the city, as groups march determinedly between stops on the tourist trail. Numerous licensed artists set up stalls along its path to tempt you with watercolours or moody black-and-white photographs.

STARÉ MĚSTO (OLD TOWN)

While political power was invested in Hradčany, the **Old Town** (Staré Město) – a cluster of streets on the opposite bank of the river – was the commercial heart of Prague. The city sat on important trading routes, east–west from Krakow into Germany and north–south from Vienna to Warsaw. As the Bohemian *groschen* became one of the major currencies in Europe, so the city began to take on a grander appearance. Today it not only offers streets full of architectural delights from the medieval to the Baroque, but is also one of the busiest parts of the city. Old Town Square, at the heart of the Old Town and once the main marketplace for the city, is a good place to embark on a visit.

The Astronomical Clock

Old Town Square

Often considered to be the very centre of Prague, **Old Town Square** (Staroměstské náměstí) is a focus for tour groups, carriage rides, bars, cafés and shopping opportunities. It is also one of the architectural highlights of the city. Of a large, irregular shape that has changed over the centuries, it is dominated in modern times by a powerful **Monument to Jan Hus** (pomník Jana Husa), unveiled in 1915 on the 500th anniversary of the martyr's death. The **Old Town Hall** (Staroměstská radnice; open Mon 11am–6pm, Tues–Sun 9am–6pm; admission charge) sits on the southwest corner of the square. A curious amalgamation of buildings in different architectural styles – its earliest elements date from the 14th century – it expanded as Prague grew in importance. Badly damaged in World War II, the north wing has only recently been restored.

Although many interesting features adorn the exterior of the building, most visitors crowd to see the **Astronomical Clock** which was added in 1490. At the time, it was so highly prized by the city fathers that they had the clockmaker who made it blinded so that he could not re-create his masterpiece. On every hour, the figures on the clock perform their ritual. Death consults his watch and pulls a cord that rings a bell; Christ and the apostles appear above; and the crowing of a cock signals the end of the proceedings. The clock captures time in a variety of ways, from the passing seconds to the cycles of the sun and moon. It is interesting to note that, in keeping with the thinking of the time, the clock shows the earth positioned at the centre of the universe.

You can visit the inside of the Old Town Hall to see the council chambers with their superb tapestries and the newly renovated Oriel Chapel. Climb the Old Town Hall Tower, erected in 1364, for an excellent view of the surrounding streets and rooftops. Abutting the Old Town Hall is **Dům U Minuty**. With its distinctive *sgraffito* decoration it is one of the most memorable Renaissance buildings in Prague.

The west flank of the square altered dramatically in the late 20th century. A large, open area behind the Old Town Hall was cleared following the devastation wreaked during the German occupation.

The House of the Minute

It now has numerous craft stalls, and benches where weary tourists can take a rest. The ornate façade of the **Church of St Nicholas** (kostel svatého Mikuláše) was once hidden down a narrow side street but today it appears as part of the north flank. Although a church has occupied this site since the 12th century, the present building dates from 1735. During World War I it was taken over as a barracks by troops of the Prussian army, and at the end of the conflict was handed over to the Hussite Church. It now functions as a concert venue during the summer season.

The east flank is dominated by two buildings. The eye-catching rococo façade belongs to **Kinský Palace** (palác Kinských), designed by Kilian Deintzenhofer and built from 1755–65 by Anselmo Lurago. In 1948, from the palace balcony, Klement Gottwald made a speech that was instrumental in the communist takeover of the government. Today, the palace contains the National Gallery's excellent collection of **Prints and Drawings**

In stark contrast is the **Church of Our Lady before Týn** (kostel Panny Marie

Church of Our Lady before Týn

před Týnem), an immense Gothic edifice whose 15th-century towers rise to 80m (260ft) above the surrounding medieval streets. The church was a hotbed of heresy from its earliest days and became the main Hussite place of worship as the reform movement grew in popularity during the 16th century. Following the Counter-Reformation, it was handed back to the Catholic Church and has remained steadfast to the present day. The church is open for Mass only (timings are posted outside), although you can peep in through the door.

Around the Square
The streets surrounding Old Town Square are a delight to explore. Almost every building throws up some highlight,

ranging from the tiniest detail – a doorknocker or carved lintel – to the grand statement, for example the superb Renaissance door of the **House at the Two Bears** (Dům u Dvou Zlatých Medvědů), on Melantrichova. There's no better way to explore this part of town than on foot, and much of the Old Town is pedestrianised, allowing you to stroll in safety.

West of Old Town Square, the area extending to the river is probably the most densely packed with fine mansions. However, it also has one of the highest concentrations of tourist shops and is often filled with people, which can spoil your ability to take in every detail. Next to Old Town Square is the much smaller **Malé náměstí**, decorated with a filigree fountain. On the east side of the square, it is the highly decorated façade of Rott House (U Rotta) that steals the show. The paintings by acclaimed 19th-century Czech artist Mikoláš Aleš have recently been restored.

Karlova or **Charles Street** is the most direct route to Charles Bridge. Look out for **Clam-Gallas Palace** (Clam-Gallasův palác), a magnificent Baroque building set with gargantuan statues by Matthia Bernard Braun. Just before you reach the river you will pass the high walls of the **Clementinum** (Klementinum), a former Jesuit college and

Execution Square

Old Town Square used to serve as a backdrop to public gatherings and also executions. In 1437, 56 Hussite soldiers mounted the scaffold. On 21 June 1621, the 27 leaders of the uprising of 1618 were executed on the order of King Ferdinand II. Their number was made up of noblemen and ordinary citizens, Germans and Czechs alike. Twenty-four of the condemned were put to death by the same executioner. The event is commemorated by a plaque set in the wall of the Old Town Hall along with crosses planted in the ground.

The Clementinum

the largest complex of buildings on this side of the river. The site saw the day as the Dominican monastery of St Clement, but was offered to the Jesuit brotherhood by Ferdinand I in 1556 to promote Catholic education. Work commenced on the Church of the Holy Saviour in 1593, and its domes now describe one of the most recognisable outlines in the city. By the middle of the 17th century the Jesuits had a monopoly on education in the city as the Hussite faculty of the Carolinum *(see page 60)* was disbanded. The Clementinum expanded as the university grew, resulting in a large part of the Old Town being demolished in 1653, although this process was not completed until one hundred years later. When the Jesuit brotherhood was dissolved by papal decree in 1773, the Clementinum became home to the library of the secular Charles University. Today it is the **National Library**, and the churches that sprang up are used as venues for concerts.

The approach to Charles Bridge is marked by the small Knights of the Cross Square (Křižovnické náměstí), watched over by a majestic statue of Charles IV erected here in 1848 to mark the 500th anniversary of the founding of Charles University. On the north side is the **Church of the Crusader Knights** dedicated to St Franciscus Seraphicus (svatého Františka Serafínského). It is the one church that is solely open for services. From here the bridge beckons, but we will remain on this bank.

South of the bridge is a small outcrop dotted with buildings. Furthest away, with a wonderful view of the river, bridge and castle is the **Smetana Museum** (muzeum Bedřicha Smetany), which pays homage to one of the Czech Republic's most beloved of composers and musicians.

South of Karlova is **Bethlehem Square** (Betlémské náměstí) where you will find a reproduction of the 14th-century **Bethlehem Chapel** (Betlémská kaple). It was here that Jan Hus embarked on his campaign to reform the Catholic Church, which ended in his execution. One main form of protest consisted in conducting Mass in Czech instead of Latin. Just around the corner from here is the **Rotunda of the Holy Cross**, the loveliest of the three remaining Romanesque round churches in Prague.

French-style Pařížská

The Jewish Quarter

The area north of Old Town Square has quite a different character from the rest of the district. This is **Josefov**, once the base of one of the most active and influential Jewish communities in Eastern Europe and still home to an orthodox community. To reach Josefov, walk down **Pařížská**, by the side of the Church of St Nicholas. This street, as the name suggests, is reminiscent of a leafy Paris boulevard complete with fine boutiques *(see page 54)*.

The Jewish community was founded in the latter years of the 11th century. Throughout the centuries the Jews were alternatively accepted and ostracised by the ruling dynasties. Certainly they were never allowed to expand beyond this small quarter. Despite a devastating fire in 1689 and the demolition of many buildings in the quarter in the 1890s to make way for new, more sanitary, housing, several important buildings were saved. In the days leading to the genocide of the Jews by the Nazis in World War II, the treasures of numerous synagogues in Bohemia were brought to Prague for safekeeping and in order that a museum might be founded to document an extinct race after German victory. The collection is now managed by the **Jewish Museum** (open Apr–Oct Sun–Fri 9am–6pm, Nov–Mar Sun–Fri 9am–4.30pm; admission charge), which oversees several museums housed in the synagogues of Josefov.

➤ The **Old-New Synagogue** (Staronová synagóga; not part of the Jewish Museum; admission charge) is the oldest surviving synagogue in Europe. Built at the beginning of the 13th century it was named the New Synagogue but renamed

A Small Corner of Paris

North of Old Town Square, Pařížská branches off to the northwest. Created over a century ago as part of an arbitrary restoration programme for the Josefov, it boasts a wealth of magnificent Art Nouveau façades. Some of Prague's trendiest hang-outs are situated in this area, notably Barock (No. 24; open daily 10am–1am), which is particularly popular among the young and the local fashion-industry crowd for its oriental cuisine; and Pravda (No. 75; open daily noon–1am), a resolutely modern restaurant whose eclectic menu has earned it its clientele base of mainly young, well-off professionals.

Old-New when a newer synagogue, now demolished, was built nearby. It is one of the finest medieval buildings in the city. The main hall is reached through a small, arched doorway featuring an elaborate carving of a vine; the 12 bunches of grapes depict the 12 tribes of Israel. The interior walls bear traces of 13th-century frescoes and later inscriptions of sections of the Psalms. The brick gables on the exterior were added in the 15th century.

The Old Jewish Cemetery bathed in delicate light

Next to the synagogue is the **Jewish Town Hall** (Židovská radnice), the seat of the Chief Rabbi. Its pink, Baroque façade is crowned by a fine tower and two clocks, which tell the time in Hebrew and Roman numerals.

The entrance to a complex of two synagogues and the Jewish Cemetery lies on Široká. The ticket office here offers a special rate for one or all of the Jewish Museum attractions; alternatively, you can buy tickets at each separate venue. At this site, the **Pinkas Synagogue** (Pinkasova synagóga) began life as a private family place of worship, although it was later expanded to rival the Old-New Synagogue. Following the end of World War II, the names of all the Czech victims of the Holocaust were inscribed on the walls of this synagogue in a stark and powerful tribute to those who lost their lives.

Make your way through the outer courtyard of the Synagogue to reach the **Old Jewish Cemetery** (Starý židovský hřbitov). This small area was once the only burial ground for Jews and as such each plot was used by several generations of the same family. It is thought that over 12,000 gravestones have been placed here, the earliest surviving ones dating from 1429 and the most recent from 1787. The jumble of carved stones sits under the shade of mature elder trees, and a dappled light plays on this peaceful resting place.

The **Klausen Synagogue** (Klausová synagóga) sits on the far side of the cemetery and was built on the ruins of a school, or *klausen*, in 1694. It displays artefacts relating to Jewish history and customs, including biographical information about the major figures of the Jewish community of Prague such as Rabbi Löw, who was suspected of working with the supernatural. His ornate tomb in the cemetery is regularly visited by well-wishers who have come to pay their respects.

The Spanish Synagogue

The Jewish Museum is responsible for two other synagogues. Nearby, **Maisel Synagogue** (Maiselova synagóga), on Maiselova, also began life as a private house of prayer – that of Mordachai Maisel who acted as banker to Emperor Rudolf II. The original structure was lost in the fire of 1689, but replaced by this ornate building, and it makes a fine backdrop to the collection of treasures it displays. Rare items of religious significance dating back to the

Renaissance, including liturgical silver, textiles and manuscripts, can be viewed here.

Finally, a comparatively recent addition to the Jewish
Museum is perhaps its *pièce de résistance*. The **Spanish
Synagogue** (Španělská synagóga), a little way east on
Vězeňská, has been renovated and its 1860s Moorish architectural style and wall decoration – reminiscent of the palace
at Alhambra in southern Spain which has given it its name –
are truly dazzling. The richness of the interior is in total contrast with the simplicity of the Old-New Synagogue.

On the Banks of the Vltava
On the outskirts of Josefov are three attractions that
are in no way associated with the Jewish community. The
Museum of Decorative Arts (Uměleckoprůmyslové muzeum) occupies a French-style neo-Classical building whose
rear overlooks the Old Jewish Cemetery. It is a showcase for
all types of decorative art, at which the Bohemians have
consistently excelled. The museum holds one of the world's
largest collections of antique glass, with many fine domestic
pieces. There are also displays relating to ceramics, tapestries, costumes and clocks.

In the direction of the river stands the impressive, neo-
Renaissance façade of the **Rudolfinum** (Dům umělců), one
of the finest concert venues in the city and home to the
Czech Philharmonic Orchestra. It served as the seat of the
Czech parliament immediately after independence in 1918.

Also on the banks of the Vltava, but a little way north, is
St Agnes's Convent (klášter svaté Anežsky). The convent
was founded in the first half of the 13th century by the Poor
Clares, and at its prime was a large complex of several churches and cloisters before falling into decay. Today
the remaining buildings have been restored to house the
National Gallery's collection of **Medieval Art in Bohemia**

and **Central Europe: 1200–1550** (open Tues–Sun 10am–6pm), including works by Master Theodoric, Lucas Cranach the Elder and Albrecht Dürer. The convent also acts as a venue for concerts and temporary exhibitions.

East of Old Town Square, beyond the Church of Our Lady before Týn, you will find a collection of narrow, historic lanes which hold the pretty **Church of St James** (kostel svatého Jakuba), and a wide thoroughfare, **Celetná**. Now a pedestrian zone, it was once the major entry route to the city from the east. A stroll along Celetná reveals many fine houses, little alleyways, courtyards and deep cellars. Faint traces of Renaissance Prague are discernible among the flowery Baroque decoration. The **House of the Black Madonna** (dům U černé Matky boží) at No. 34 dates from the early 20th century. The huge windows of this Cubist masterpiece, built by Josef Gočár in 1911–12, reveal its original use as a department store. The statue after which the house is named is located in a niche set on the corner of the façade. Completely renovated in 1994, the building is now home to the National Gallery's **Museum of Czech Cubism** (open Tues–Sun 10am–6pm).

The Royal Route

The Powder Gate marked the start of the so-called Royal Route, the route which the coronation processions of the Bohemian kings and queens took through the city, and which linked Royal Court Palace and Hradčany Castle across the river.

Carriages would travel down Celetná, through Old Town Square and along Karlova, before heading across Charles Bridge. Once in Malá Strana they would travel along Mosteká into Lesser Quarter Square before making their way via Nerudova to St Vitus Cathedral in the castle compound. There, the new monarch would be crowned.

At the eastern end of the street is the **Powder Gate** (Prašná brána), a tower dating from the end of the 13th century. It was one of a number of gates into the Old Town and marked a transition from the previously favoured defensive structure to a ceremonial entranceway. Originally, it was linked to a palace, called the Royal Court, which was demolished at the beginning of the 20th century after lying derelict for a number of decades. In its place – in the manner of a phoenix rising from its ashes – is one of Prague's foremost Art Nouveau buildings, the **Municipal House** (Obecní dům).

The Municipal House

The complex was planned and built in the first decade of the 20th century to provide new exhibition space as well as a modern auditorium located at the heart of the building. The Municipal House was one of the first buildings in Prague to be renovated, the result causing controversy in architectural circles. Its auditorium, **Smetana Hall**, is well established as one of the major arts venues in the city, and there is a fine Art Nouveau café on the ground floor.

From Powder Gate, come back into the Old Town and one street south of Celetná is Železná, also pedestrianised. Halfway down the street you will immediately see the wrought-iron adornment of the **Estates Theatre** (Stavovské divadlo) ahead. Built in the 1780s, in its lines are some of the finest examples of neo-Classical architecture in the city and it formed the centrepiece of social activity in Prague when it opened. Here on 29 October 1878, Mozart conducted the premiere of his new opera *Don Giovanni* in front of a rapturous audience. The theatre rekindled its relationship with Mozart when it was used as a set for the film *Amadeus*, directed by Czech Miloš Forman.

Next to the theatre lie the remains of the first university of Prague. The **Carolinum** (Karolinum) was founded by Charles IV and named after him. Jan Hus held the post of rector here and the campus became a hotbed of Hussite activity. After the victory of the Counter-Reformation it was handed over to the Catholic Jesuits and merged with their Clementinum complex near the river. Much of what remains here dates from the 18th century, but look for the beautiful oriel window overhanging the street between the Carolinum and Estates Theatre.

NOVÉ MĚSTO (THE NEW TOWN)

Charles IV gave the go-ahead for the building of the New Town (Nové Město) in 1348 when overcrowding in the Old Town was becoming an acute problem. Although much of the first stage of building has been swept away in subsequent redevelopment, the New Town has many important attractions. It is also a focus for hotels, and entertainment in the form of theatres, nightclubs and cinemas.

Na příkopě is the street that was the traditional dividing line between the Old Town and the New Town. It was built over the old moat, the defensive structure around the Old Town and links to the Powder Gate at its eastern end. Today it is pedestrianised, and is one of Prague's most important retail streets, lined with modern shops, restaurants, casinos and exchange offices. The Prague Information Service office can be found at No. 20.

The south end of Na příkopě meets **Wenceslas Square** (Václavské náměstí), the symbolic heart of modern Prague for independent Czechoslovakia and the Czech Republic. The scale of the square is truly impressive: more of a boulevard than a plaza, at first glance it brings to mind the Champs-Elysées in Paris. Huge crowds have gathered here in times of joy and sorrow, most recently in 1968 to protest against the arrival of Russian troops, and in 1989 to cheer the fall of communism. From Na příkopě there is a slight uphill slope which gives way to the extraordinary vista at its southeastern end.

Wenceslas Square by night, watched over by the Good King

Closed to through-traffic, the square is a popular place for a stroll. Nowhere else in the city will you find as many hotels, restaurants, shops, cinemas, cafés, bars and nightclubs as here.

Pride of place still goes to the **Café Evropa**, an Art Nouveau gem with a terrace where you can watch the world wander by. The hotel to which it belongs was once the toast of the city and retains a certain faded splendour. Also look out for the Wiehl House with its Art Nouveau decoration by Mikoláš Aleš on the corner of Vodičková.

At the top of the square sits the **St Wenceslas Monument**, crowned by a statue of the saint astride a noble steed. Below the great man are life-size statues of the other patron saints of the former Czechoslovakia. The work of Josef Myslbek, it is perhaps one of the best-known images of the city and was erected in 1912. Near the immense monument is another monument, simpler yet very poignant, commemorating the **Czech victims of the Communist regime**. In 1969, two young Czechs set themselves alight in the square in protest of the Russian intervention to end the 'Prague Spring'. This memorial, although focusing on their fate, stands for all those who suffered or died under the regime.

At the head of Wenceslas Square is the **National Museum** (Národní muzeum). Created at a time of rising national consciousness in the late 1890s, its neo-Renaissance styling makes a confident statement with a beautifully decorated exterior and grand interior. The museum contains dull collections relating to mineralogy, archaeology and anthropology.

North of the museum along Wilsonova – always busy with traffic – is the **State Opera** (Státní opera), neo-Classical in design. Beyond this is the main railway station built in Art Nouveau style, although now looking a little worse for wear.

Just north of the square on Panská 7 is the concise and excellent **Mucha Museum** (open daily 10am–6pm; admission charge), dedicated to the beautiful Art Nouveau works of Alphonse Mucha; there's also a very good gift shop attached.

From Wenceslas Square, the bulk of the New Town lies to the southwest between the busy Šokolská and the river. Starting at the northwest end of Wenceslas Square and heading towards the Vltava you will come to **Jungmannova**. This is now one of the prime shopping areas of the city, spilling over with department stores, upmarket galleries and exclusive boutiques.

On the north side of Jungmannova Square (Jungmannovo náměstí) is the **Church of Our Lady of the Snows** (kostel Panny Marie Sněžné); look out for a curious Cubist lamppost outside the northwest entrance. Founded by Charles IV to mark his coronation in 1347 the intention was for the structure to comprise three aisles, but work was interrupted by the Hussite uprising. What remains today is the chancel of the original plan, standing on its own and consequently looking completely out of scale in relation to its floor area.

The National Theatre and Vicinity

Follow Národni in the direction of the river to find the **National Theatre** (Národní divadlo) and the New National ◄ Theatre. The former, an impressive building that adds grace to the riverfront vista, was built in the middle of the 19th century as the result of an undercurrent of demand for an independent theatre. In 1881, just before the theatre was due to open, it was completely destroyed by an accidental fire. However, such was the level of national pride at the time that within weeks the money had been raised to rebuild it. Many

The neoclassical roof of the National Theatre

of the finest Czech artists of their day were commissioned to work on the theatre, which was renovated in the 1980s when Karel Prager was commissioned to design the New National Theatre so as to expand the complex. It is one of the most striking examples of modern architecture in the city, presenting three cubic buildings with façades of glass brick, and acts as a permanent home to the National Theatre Company and Lanterna Magika.

Architecture Old and New

When you come to the river you will see the **Slovanský ostrov** island to your left. The island did not exist until the early 1700s, but, following work to shore up its banks, it became the centre of social life in the city. Here, the distinctive Renaissance tower is linked to the Manés Gallery. This edifice in the Bauhaus style is one of the best examples of functionalism that Prague has to offer. The headquarters of the Manés group of artists who take their name from the

---

Memories of the Resistance

On 18 June 1942, the Church of St Cyril and St Methodius became the scene of an unequal battle between the assassins of the Nazi governor of Bohemia and Moravia, Reinhard Heydrich, and the SS. The members of the Resistance had sought refuge in the crypt after throwing a bomb at Heydrich's open-top car, and barricaded themselves in. However, their hiding place was betrayed and German troops 350 strong circled the church. Despite their best efforts, it took them over six hours to break through the defences, during which time 14 of the combatants were killed and many dozen more injured. When the Germans finally did gain access, they were unable to take a single prisoner: all of the Resistance fighters had either perished in the battle or chosen to take their own lives rather than surrender.

The 'dancing' towers of the Fred and Ginger Building

19th-century artistic dynasty, it has a changing programme of avant-garde exhibitions.

Further south down Masarykovo nábřeží (Masaryk riverside boulevard), on the corner of Resslova, is another fine example of modern architecture. The **Tančící dům**, or dancing building, was designed by American architect Frank Gehry in the early 1990s and has become known locally as the Fred and Ginger Building. A flowing glass-and-concrete tower (Ginger) gives the impression of being held by the upright tower that is Fred, as if caught in action on the dance floor.

Walk down Resslova to find the **Church of St Cyril and St Methodius** (kostel svatého Cyrila a Metoděje). Methodius, regarded as the father of Czech Christianity, was ably accompanied by St Cyril in his mission to preach the gospel. Built in the Baroque period (c.1730), this church was originally dedicated to St Charles Borromeo and served retired priests. It closed in 1783 but in the 1930s was reopened under the auspices of the Czech Orthodox Church, hence the change of name. The church became embroiled in one of the tragic episodes of World War II when, after they had assassinated the brutal Nazi governor Reinhard Heydrich, his killers sought refuge in the crypt *(see box page 64)*. The plan had been hatched without the approval of the Czech Resistance movement and the repercussions were disastrous: the Nazis exacted horrific revenge by ordering the village of Lidice on the outskirts of Prague to be burnt to the ground, the men shot, and the women and some of the children deported to concentration camps. A small memorial is to be found outside the church where bullet holes from the incident can still be seen. Inside, the crypt has been turned into a memorial museum (open Tues–Sun 10am–4pm) with photographs, documents and memorabilia of the event.

The 15th-century tower of the New Town Hall

The east end of Resslova meets **Charles Square** (Karlovo náměstí), the largest in the city. Laid out in the original city plan of 1348, it was in its beginnings the biggest market in Prague and was known as the Cattle Market. In the mid-19th century the square was transformed with the creation of a garden area, which today offers a place for local city dwellers to relax. The surrounding apartment blocks are not particularly exciting but **Faust House** (Faustův dům) has been preserved and refurbished. The history of the house, which was given its baroque appearance in the 18th century, stretches back to the 14th century, when it belonged to Prince Václav of Opava, an alchemist and natural historian. In the 16th century, it was home to Englishman Edward Kelley, charged by Emperor Rudolf II with turning base metal into gold. The many secretive practices carried out here fostered its association with the legend of Faust.

> **Dvořák composed an impressive number of works in his lifetime: 31 pieces of chamber music, 50 orchestra scores and nine symphonies, including the famous *Slavic Dances*.**

Walking north towards the Old Town you will find the **New Town Hall** (Novoměstská radnice) at the end of Charles Square. Building work started in 1348, and in 1419 it was the site of the First Defenestration of Prague *(see page 16)*. Several additions were made in the 16th and 18th centuries, but it is the 15th-century tower that is still the building's crowning glory.

Before strolling back into the main part of the town, take a detour to **U Fleků** on Křemencová. This is probably Prague's most authentic beer hall and has been open since 1499. It only serves the strong dark beer brewed on its premises – it is the smallest brewery in the city – and patrons sit at long tables in traditional wood-panelled drinking rooms. You can also sample the Czech cooking and enjoy a nightly cabaret performance.

Close to the I.P. Pavlova metro station is the Baroque **Villa Amerika**, completed in 1720. Designed by Kilian Ignaz Dienzenhofer, it was originally used by the Michna family as a summer palace. Today it houses the **Dvořák Museum** (muzeum Antonína Dvořáka; open Tues–Sun 10am–5pm), with memorabilia relating to one of the greatest

Czech composers. There are live recitals during the summer, although recorded compositions by Dvořák are played when the musicians are not present.

Around the corner, at No. 12 Na bojišti, is the **Chalice Restaurant** (U Kalicha), famous for being the favourite drinking hall of the writer Jaroslav Hašek, creator of the celebrated book, *The Good Soldier Svejk*.

OUTLYING AREAS

The suburbs of Prague have a preponderance of dour modern apartment blocks to house the growing population. However, there are a number of attractions that make a trip out on the metro or tram well worth the effort.

St Martin's Rotunda

Vyšehrad

Vyšehrad (Vyšehrad metro station), meaning high castle, has an important place in the Czech national psyche. On this rocky mound overlooking the Vltava, the legendary Přemyslid Princess Libuše foretold the founding of a great city on the banks of the river. She is said to have married a common man and begotten the children who would become the founders of the Czech nation. Unfortunately for the legends, archaeological activity can only date the settlement here to the 10th century, making it younger than Prague Castle.

The castle was built *c.*1085 by the Přemyslid leader Vratislav II and his two successors, who sought to consolidate power within their growing kingdoms. Along with the castle, an abbey was also built, and later a Romanesque basilica. Power was transferred to Prague Castle by the end of the 12th century, however Charles IV

The elaborate doorway of the Church of Saints Peter and Paul

breathed new life into Vyšehrad with new fortifications and large mansions in homage to his mother, who was descended from the Přemyslid dynasty. During the Hussite uprising many of the fortifications were destroyed, to be rebuilt in the late 17th century — these are the walls we see today.

From the metro station, a short walk will lead through Baroque **Leopold Gate** (Leopoldova brána) and on to a simple stone church. This is **St Martin's Rotunda** (rotunda svatého Martina), one of the oldest churches in Bohemia. Built in the 11th century, it was never extended or replaced, although it was restored in the late 1800s.

Make your way to the neo-Gothic **Church of Saints Peter and Paul** (kostel svatého Petr a Pavel), which was erected on the site of earlier places of worship. At this time, Vyšehrad's mythical status as the birthplace of the Czech nation was once more gaining favour thanks to a blossoming spirit of nationalism. It was decided that the cemetery here would become a **national cemetery** for illustrious Czechs, a symbol of national pride. The cemetery has some fine sculptures carved by masters of their art, and the

The transport section of the National Technical Museum merits a visit

composers Antonín Dvořák and Bedřich Smetana, along with the poet Jan Neruda, are among the luminaries who rest here.

National Technical Museum

The **National Technical Museum** (Národní Technické muzeum), housed in a rather plain 1930s building (tram routes 1, 8, 25 and 26), hides a wealth of machinery relating to man's technical achievements. There are sections on astronomy, cinematography and industry, the latter illustrated by a fully re-created coal mine. However, the main focus of the museum resides in its colossal 'History of Transport' section. Here you will find cars, trains and aeroplanes dating from the days when motorised transport was still in its infancy. Czech-made examples feature particularly prominently.

The Museum of Modern and Contemporary Art

Founded in 1995 in the **Trades Fair Palace** (Veletržní palác; tram routes 5, 17), a masterpiece of 1920s architecture, the National Gallery's collection of **Modern and Contemporary Art** showcases work from the 19th and 20th centuries. The redesigned interior of the palace offers a contemporary viewing environment very suited to its collection. Although the works of Czech artists such as Mikoláš Aleš – who was at the forefront of the 'generation of the National Theatre' group – feature prominently, its draw for foreign visitors may well be its French collection.

The collection was brought together with the precise aim of representing the major transitions of French art. Many of the works on show were purchased by the Czech State in the 1920s. Each major modern school or artist figures here, from the Barbizon School to influential Cubist works by Picasso and Braque. The museum also has works by Gauguin, Cézanne and Delacroix, along with a range of Impressionist canvasses.

In the early 20th century, Prague's influence on the arts, photography and architecture was considerable and the gallery offers an interesting exposition of the exponents of each genre.

The Exhibition Ground and Stromovka Park

Stromovka (Výstaviště a Stromovka; tram routes 5, 17) was for many centuries a royal hunting ground before being designated a public park in 1804. Today its woodland and lakes provide a pleasant alternative to the sometimes hot and dusty city streets. The **Exhibition Ground** was chosen as the location for the Jubilee of 1891, and its large buildings still host regular exhibitions, concerts and events. A huge summer funfair also pulls in a crowd made up of visitors with children and Prague's young people alike.

Mozart Museum

Bertramka (tram routes 4, 7, 9) was the villa where Mozart stayed on numerous occasions during his visits to Prague. It sits on a wooded expanse of land, which in his time would have been quite removed from the hubbub of the city. In 1787 during one of his visits, Mozart composed elements of the opera *Don Giovanni* only hours before the work's debut at the Estates Theatre. The small museum here displays letters and scores in the hand of the great man, along with a number of musical instruments. In summer there are recitals in the courtyard, which adds an extra dimension to your visit.

Letná Park

Set on the banks of the Vltava opposite the Jewish Quarter, **Letná Park** (Letenské sady) is another open space within easy reach of the city. Not as well managed as the Petřín area, it is nevertheless worth a visit for the superb views upriver and across the Old Town that its southern edge offers. Visitors are also drawn to a strange modern sculpture that sits on a concrete plinth overlooking the Vltava. The constantly swaying arm of a giant metronome was installed here after the Velvet Revolution, replacing a huge statue of Stalin that was blown up after the Russian dictator's death. The metronome may have its critics, but it certainly succeeds in being a talking point.

Troja Palace

Situated to the north of the city on the banks on the Vltava is the huge **Troja Palace** (Trojský zámek; Holešovice metro station then bus route 112; open Tues–Sun 10am–6pm; admission fee). Constructed by the architect Jean-Baptiste Mathey as a summer home for the Sternberg family from 1679–85, the palace became the fashionable place in which to be seen upon its completion. Designed in the classic Italianate style, it has stunning frescoes adorning its interior, the ones in the Grand Hall being particularly impressive. Among the figures depicted are Hapsburg emperors Rudolf I and Leopold I. The gardens sloping down to the river were in the French style, an innovation in Prague. Both house and garden were restored in the 1990s to original designs, and the palace now houses the collection of the Prague **City Gallery**, which includes works from the finest Czech artists of the 19th century.

The restored Troja Palace is now home to the City Gallery

Žižkov

Take metro line A to Jiřího z Poděbrad station, and you will emerge in the lively, working-class quarter of **Žižkov**, somewhat dingy in places but full of atmosphere and historical charm. Nearby is the **Church of the Sacred Heart**, built in 1932, which has a distinctive, tombstone-shaped clocktower. Behind the church, turn left on Milešovská Street to be confronted by the gargantuan **Television Tower** (open 10am–11pm). Construction began in the communist era and was completed in 1992. For a spectacular view of the city you can ascend 93m (305ft) of the 216-m (709-ft) tower to the **observation deck**.

EXCURSIONS

A day trip from Prague will allow you to discover much of the western part of the Czech Republic. Sights dotted across the Bohemian countryside include medieval towns, as yet untouched by redevelopment or over-zealous renovation, plus fine royal fortresses and hunting lodges. For those who do not wish to hire a car, several companies offer a range of morning or day trips by bus. Their programme of tours is sure to include the destinations listed below.

Karlštejn Castle

Charles IV, Holy Roman Emperor and responsible for the transformation of Prague into a sparkling capital city, was blessed with an immense personal fortune. Although Prague Castle formed the centre of his court, Charles wanted somewhere secure to keep his treasures – which numbered the crown jewels and valuable holy relics such as thorns from the crown of Christ and a tooth belonging to John the Baptist. He commissioned the building of **Karlštejn Castle** (hrad Karlštejn), 28km (17 miles) southwest of Prague, in 1348. Both Matthias of Arras and Peter Parler were involved in its construction.

They could not have selected a better site. Karlštejn is ingeniously tucked away in a narrow valley and would not have been visible to passing raiders. The sole route of access lay through the valley, which made it easy to defend. Today it is probably the most popular day trip from Prague, and thousands of visitors flock there each week. However, no tourist traffic is allowed up into the valley, and vehicles must be left in the parking area at the foot of the hill. A 15- to 20-minute walk will take you up to the castle entrance.

From the village below, your first view of the castle's walls and turrets reveal Karlštejn in all its glory. With its high,

Karlštejn Castle is a prime example of a medieval fortress

crenellated walls interspersed with lookout towers, it lives up to everyone's idea of a medieval fortress. However, it could not keep up with the evolution in methods of warfare that preceded the Thirty Years' War, and suffered terrible damage when faced with the more modern field artillery of the Swedish forces. It was not until the 19th century that repair and renovation work was undertaken, which some critics feel was overdone.

After entering the castle you will find yourself in Burgrave's Courtyard, the starting point for the guided tour. In the Imperial Palace are contained the private apartments of the emperor and empress, along with the Great Hall, used for entertaining and royal court functions. The decoration in each room is splendid, incorporating fine panelling and Gothic ceiling detail. Exhibitions revolve around the life of Charles and his lasting influence on Bohemian society.

The **Marian Tower**, or Tower of Our Lady, rising up above the palace, has two important churches. The **Church**

of Our Lady reveals some exceptional 14th-century frescoes, although it is said that many were lost in the course of the 19th-century renovations. One panel clearly shows Charles himself being handed several holy relics, including the holy thorns. A short corridor from the church leads to the tiny **St Catherine's Chapel**. This was the emperor's private retreat where he would spend time in contemplation. It is encrusted with semiprecious stones, and a portrait above the door shows Charles, dressed in a gold cloak and crown, with his second wife, Anna.

The castle **keep**, or great tower, contains the most precious treasure: the **Chapel of the Holy Cross**, reopened after decades of painstaking restoration, is the Czech Republic's answer to the Sistine Chapel. However, admission is limited and it is best to book ahead (tel: 274 008 154). It was here that the holy relics were kept, tended by a few chosen priests. The decoration in the chapel, one of the most important holy places in the Christian Empire during the 14th century, is exquisite. The walls are set with 2,451 precious and semiprecious stones (topazes, amethysts, jasper, onyx and chrysolite) and covered with over 100 portraits of saints painted by Master Theodoric, the king's painter, in the 14th century. The ceiling shimmers with gold leaf.

Kutná Hora

Kutná Hora was the second most important town in Bohemia in medieval times. A healthy seam of silver found nearby fostered its rise in status and helped to make Bohemia one of the richest states in the world. However, when the silver ran out in the 16th century, time stood still for the city. Numerous listed buildings are scattered over the centre of town and an increasing number of visitors come to enjoy its unspoiled character. The atmosphere is relaxed and genteel and you will find several places to stop for a leisurely lunch.

The centre of the old town used to be called the Royal Mint, or Italian Court due to the number of Italian artisans employed here. They were considered the most skilled in the art of coin design, to which end the silver mined here was mostly intended. The precious ore funded the building and development of the town, and of course lined the royal coffers back in Prague. The building was completed in 1300 and was designed with fortified walls and an internal courtyard. In addition to protecting the silver, the court also doubled as a royal palace in which the king would stay when he came to supervise the mint-

The Cathedral of St Barbara, Gothic masterpiece of Kutná Hora

ing process. Until recently, the building played host to the town hall but now houses a small museum.

Nearby, the Mining Museum is housed in **Hrádek**, a partly Gothic structure. In the garden is the entrance to medieval excavations where you can follow tunnels for almost 50m (55 yards).

From Hrádek, the road climbs the hill along Barborská, punctuated with beautiful statues and offering sweeping views across the Bohemian countryside. To your right is the long, elegant façade of the Jesuit seminary, the largest outside of Prague. Directly ahead is outlined the jewel in Kutná Hora's crown, the magnificent **Cathedral of St Barbara** (chrám svaté ◀

Barbory; admission charge). Begun in the 14th century from designs by Jan Parler, son of Peter, work was almost complete by the 16th century. The structure represents one of the finest and most dramatic examples of the Gothic style. However, the final plans for the church had to be altered due to the succession of architects and funding problems, which explains why some elements date from as late as the 19th century.

The exterior features a tall chancel supported by numerous flying buttresses. Three steeples shaped almost like the roofs of Bedouin tents rise above the buttresses. Inside, Parler's trademark vaulting is apparent in the chancel and nave. A chapel dedicated to Jan Smíšek, the administrator of the Royal Mines who was buried here in 1512, has fresco murals featuring the mining and minting activities so fundamental to the daily life and prosperity of the town. The cathedral was used as a set during the filming of *Les Misérables*, when it took the place of Notre-Dame Cathedral in Paris.

Karlovy Vary

Throughout the 18th and 19th centuries, Bohemia was one of the world's most visited regions. **Karlovy Vary** (Karlsbad), 130km (80 miles) west of Prague, and its sister town Mariánské Lásně (Marienbad) greatly contributed to its popularity. Both are spa towns and their waters are believed to have therapeutic qualities.

While out on a hunting trip in the neighbouring forests, Charles IV supposedly found the source of the water when a deer he was pursuing, finding itself cornered on the edge of a precipice, leapt in desperation into one of the hot pools below. The town was christened Karlsbad in Charles's honour – Karlovy Vary being the Czech equivalent of the German name.

The Hapsburg Court came here to relax, and the new wealth followed their lead. Karlsbad was the ultimate high-class resort of its time, with every modern amenity made available to its patrons – who included Czar Peter the Great and the composers Bach, Brahms and Grieg. Even philosophers such as Marx occasionally felt the need to lavish attention on the body as well as the mind. Karlsbad's visitors had often been prescribed spa treatments by their doctors, and many came to escape the pollution of the newly industrialised cities.

Today, 12 hot springs have been located in the area, the most famous one being Vřídlo or 'the bubbly one'. The fashionable set and the glitterati may have

Find a moment to relax under Karlovy Vary's elegant colonnades

turned their backs on Karlovy Vary, but the town still prides itself on providing relaxing breaks for those with taste and money, who gather to take to the waters in its luxurious surroundings. A stroll through the pedestrianised streets reveals some architectural gems and a pretty riverside promenade. You can also sit and unwind in the shade of the graceful wrought-iron colonnades. The town has a robust cultural scene – another legacy of its sophisticated past – featuring a major film festival, plays and concerts. Fortunes have been made and lost in its casinos, and there are golf courses on hand for those who just cannot keep away from the green.

Karlovy Vary is also a centre for the production of porcelain and glass; and the only place in the world to make the potent aperitif *Becherovka*, an alcoholic concoction of herbs which locals have humorously named 'the 13th healing spring'.

Marianbad, now **Mariánské Lázně**, nestles in dense woodland to the south of Karlovy Vary. There are well over 100 springs here and an array of 19th-century baths and sanatoria where you can enjoy the full benefits of the waters. As with Karlovy Vary, a range of summer concerts and shows help take your mind off the slightly sulphurous taste of the water while transporting you back to the elegant heyday of the Austro-Hungarian Empire.

České Budějovice

One hundred and forty kilometres (90 miles) south of Prague is the beautiful 13th-century settlement of **České Budějovice**. Set aside an entire day for this excursion, which takes you through the undulating landscape of fields and forests that blanket southern Bohemia. The town was said to have been founded by Otakar II, and its medieval square, reputed to be the largest of its type in the world, is framed by beautiful Renaissance and Baroque houses. Czech poet Jan Neruda described it as 'the Florence of Bohemia'. Whereas Prague's houses now glimmer with new paintwork and renovated carvings, the buildings here still wear the patina of age. Being able to wander in relative solitude adds an extra dimension to the atmosphere. Look out for highlights such as the **Dominican Monastery**, founded in 1265, and the town's former arsenal, built in 1530. Beer has been brewed here since the 16th century and the town gives its name to the famous Budvar or Budweis beer. For a refreshing pint, visit Masné Krámy; built in the 16th century as the meat market, it now houses the town's most popular beer hall.

The main square of České Budějovice, possibly the largest medieval square in the world

From the top of the Black Tower (Černá věž) it is possible to catch a glimpse of nearby **Hluboká Castle**. This 19th-century fortress is unique in Bohemia in that it has the appearance of a cake decorated with white icing. A castle has stood here since the 12th century, taken over in the 16th century by the Schwarzenberg family; it was Johann Adolf Schwarzenberg who effectuated the changes visible to this day. Inspired by the fashion for English gardens, he decided to create one in the very heart of the Bohemian countryside. Inside the house are displayed assorted weaponry and walls decked in fine Flemish tapestries. You can also view the family's collection of Bohemian art in the converted stable block.

To the south, the small town of **Český Krumlov**, with the second-largest castle in the Czech Republic, has been designated one of the UNESCO World Heritage Sites.

Konopiště Castle

In the early 20th century, the Austro-Hungarian throne passed to Archduke Franz Ferdinand, a man who had provoked the displeasure of his family by making a love match with a commoner.

The couple made their home at a 13th-century castle in **Konopiště** – a building that the archduke had purchased in 1887. Located far from the royal court in Vienna, the couple spent many idyllic years here with their children. However, in 1914 the archduke and his wife were assassinated in Sarajevo, and Europe hurtled into the bloodbath of World War I.

Konopiste Castle was once home to Archduke Franz Ferdinand

The castle (hrad Konopiště) is worth a visit for the insight it allows into the life of this extraordinary couple. It is also of note for its banqueting hall, with two Gobelin tapestries from Paris and sketches made for Cervantes' *Don Quixote*. The castle grounds feature rose gardens and ponds.

Plzeň

With its population of 180,000, **Plzeň** (Pilsen) is the Czech Republic's second-largest city. Lying 150km (95 miles) to the west of Prague, at the confluence of four rivers and at the crossroads of four trading routes, it quickly established itself as a centre of commerce.

However, Plzeň is first and foremost the cradle of Pilsen lager, the best in the land and exported to the four corners of the globe. Although the Prazdroj Brewery was only established in 1842, the city's brewing tradition is of far longer standing. When the city was founded in 1290, it was granted the right to brew its own beer. The **Museum of Beer Brewing** (Pivorvarské muzeum; open Sept–May Tues–Sun, daily Jun–Aug), the most ancient of its kind in the world, is housed in a neo-Gothic building on Veleslavínova and pays hommage to the energy that drove the industry forwards in the Middle Ages. The Prazdroj Brewery organises guided tours in English and German, daily at 12.30pm and 2pm (no need to book).

Another classic in Plzeň's industrial portfolio is the Škoda empire, manufacturers of the car by the same name. Founded in the 19th century by Emil von Škoda, the firm remained for many years the town's largest employer.

Plzeň's core is in its Square of the Republic (náměstí Republiky). In the middle of the square, the **Gothic Church of St Bartholomew** (kostel svatého Bartoloměje) projects its spire – the tallest in the country – 100 metres (333 ft) into the sky. Its interior boasts frescoes dating back to 1400.

The **Town Hall** was constructed between 1554–58 and its façade displays some fine *sgraffito*.

Ribbed vault, St Bartholomew's

Finally, the **Franciscan Monastery** (Františkánský klášter), which is situated on the southwest corner of the square, conceals the pretty Chapel of St Barbara, decorated with Gothic frescoes vividly illustrating the life of the saints.

WHAT TO DO

Prague is bursting at the seams with things to do, even after the museums and galleries have shut. Highbrow pursuits rival opportunities for more frivolous entertainment. Whether you choose to bask in the city's rich musical heritage or simply enjoy a glass of pilsner in one of its legendary beer cellars, this is one city where there really is something for everyone.

CITY TOURS

Prague is a city tailor-made for tours, with a wealth of pretty views, historic buildings, religious icons and famous inhabitants. There are a plethora of walking tours to choose from, some covering the general history of the city while others home in on specific themes – the history of the Jewish community, Romanesque Prague, Gothic Prague, Baroque Prague, Renaissance Prague or Composers' Prague. You can join a group or book your own personal guide. Registered guides are founts of knowledge about their city and their enthusiasm is definitely infectious. Contact Prague Information Service for details of registered guides *(see page 128).*

> Jiři Koláři is one of the best Czech artists alive today, known for his collages and 'visual poems'. He and his wife have opened the Jiřiho a Běly Kolářovi Gallery (14 Betlémské Náměstí; open daily 9am–6pm), which shows his work and that of emerging Czech artists.

If the idea of walking does not appeal to you, you can always blend culture with comfort by taking a ride through

Marionettes come in hundreds of different characters

Prague instead. Horse-drawn carriages carry you at a gentle pace through the cobbled streets of the Old Town; or opt for a ride in a vintage car – open-top, weather permitting. Both tours depart from Old Town Square. Riverboats operating day or evening cruises ply the waters of the Vltava, with candlelit dinners and jazz bands for added interest. Boarding takes place on the Lesser Quarter bank just below Charles Bridge.

During the summer months, Prague's historic tram 91 tours the city. The National Theatre, Malostranská náměstí and Wenceslas Square are all boarding points.

ENTERTAINMENT

Prague is home to a multitude of theatre, ballet and opera companies, with a strong tradition of puppetry and mime. However, it is undoubtedly in the field of classical music that it has established itself as a world leader, as its wealth of concert venues and its packed musical programme will testify.

Kafka, Back in the Limelight

Like a great number of the central figures in the history of Prague, Franz Kafka spoke German. This factor lost him the support of the Czech public when the country rid itself once and for all of Austro-Hungarian state supervision in 1918, and again in 1945 when the German minority was expelled. The author of *The Castle*, *The Trial* and *The Metamorphosis* was equally banished by the communist regime for being a bourgeois intellectual.

Kafka finally seems to be back in fashion. The place of his birth at U Radnice 5 has borne his name since 2000, and a small exhibition (open Tues–Fri 10am–6pm, Sat 10am–5pm) reveals his life and work. The new Franz Kafka museum (Cihelná 2b; open daily 10am–6pm; admission charge) uses multimedia displays to explore the writer's background, emphasising the influence of personal experiences on his books.

Music and Theatre

The city has been a major concert venue for at least five centuries. It greeted the premiere of Mozart's *Don Giovanni* and the Hapsburg Court played host to numerous major composers during their careers. Large concert halls have been built during various periods in the history of Prague and today, along with a host of smaller venues, they arrange concerts all year long.

Dvořák's works top the bill in Prague's concert halls

Orchestras of international stature appear at venues such as the **Rudolfinum** (tel: 227 059 111) or **Smetana Hall** at the Municipal House (tel: 222 002 121). Lesser-known touring outfits or smaller groups, for example quartets, perform at the **Clementinum** or **St Nicholas Church** to name but a few venues.

Throughout the year large-scale festivals devote themselves to the work of particular composers or specific musical styles. Favoured composers include Mozart, Vivaldi, Bach and Verdi, although Czech heroes such as Dvořák and Smetana are not forgotten. Concerts are held at lunchtime and in the evening and you can purchase seats from the ticket sellers in Old Town Square. Alternatively, head to the box office of the venue in question. With ticket prices representing such good value there is the potential to see a different performance each day – and many people do just that.

The city is also home to the Czech National Theatre, ballet and opera companies, and regularly welcomes touring

One of Prague's numerous puppet theatres displays its quirky sign

groups. The **National Theatre** (tel: 224 901 668) is an enormous complex with several stages, and encompasses the national opera and ballet companies. It also includes the **Laterna Magika** (tel: 222 222 041), one of the major European troupes and at the forefront of multimedia theatre. This popular genre blends music, mime, ballet surrealism and satire into a powerful melange that transcends the language barrier. Each season, **Estates Theatre** (tel: 224 902 322) also plays host to several companies, and the **State Opera** (tel: 224 227 266) stages seminal opera, ballet and dance productions.

Marionette performances take place at the **National Marionette Theatre** (tel: 224 819 322). Watch the puppets run the gamut of emotions in sophisticated plays of a more serious bent, or clown around in light-hearted pieces. Complete listings of what's on during your stay in the city are included in the English-language *Prague Post* newspaper.

Nightlife

If cultural overload strikes, why not seek refuge in Prague's plethora of bars and cafés where you can enjoy a few drinks and listen to live rock, jazz or folk music. For a glass of local beer nowhere beats one of the city's huge beer cellars, complete with roving accordion players. However, on a warm summer's evening, try to find a bar terrace with a view over the city and watch the swallows swooping over the rooftops as the sun sets. This really is one of the most beautiful and romantic cities in the world, so take time to savour the atmosphere.

As the evening wears on, Prague's lively nightlife kicks in. Trends can be short-lived, so follow the local crowds for the hippest nightclubs. However, for a relatively safe bet head for Prague's most long-standing club, **Radost FX** (Bělehradská 120, Prague 2; tel: 224 254 776; metro station I.P. Pavlova). Still very stylish, this venue attracts the cream of the local DJs, not to mention international guest DJs, and holds a gay night once a week.

SHOPPING

The 1990s saw huge changes in how and where people shopped in the city. This is one area where Prague has completely broken away from its communist past of limited goods in state-owned department stores. Today, shopping here is an experience just as exciting as in any other European city, with an array of quality goods and traditional handicrafts.

The main shopping streets boast the flagship stores of all the well-known, international chains. However, by venturing into the Old Town you will come across small, specialist shops where you can browse for hours.

Do remember to check whether stores take credit cards. Although payment by credit card is widespread, it is by no means universally accepted.

Where to Shop

The majority of the souvenir shops can be found along the 'royal way' leading from Municipal House through the Old Town Square, and in Lesser Quarter Square across the river. With so many shops selling crystal, porcelain, garnet jewellery and crafts you can easily compare prices and quality before you buy. Big names from the (Western) high street have set up shop around Wenceslas Square and along Na příkopě, whereas on the more up-market streets of Pařížská and Jungmannova, European *haute couture* rubs shoulders with the emerging Czech designer labels.

One of the many souvenir stands by Prague Castle

Markets are an interesting alternative. Among the wares in the craft market next to the Old Town Hall are marionettes, wrought-iron pieces fashioned while you wait, and the ubiquitous tourist T-shirts. The daily street market on Havelská has some souvenir stalls but focuses on fresh produce.

Finally, Charles Bridge is perhaps one of the most romantic shopping venues anywhere. Few can resist buying something from one of the many stalls as they drink in the incredible views.

What to Buy

The Czech Republic has a high reputation for the quality of many of its traditional products. Glasswear and porcelain are particularly renowned and examples of both are to be found in royal collections all across Europe. **Bohemian Crystal** remains an exclusive brand name despite having factories scattered throughout the country. Lead crystal ranges in lead content from 14 percent to 24 percent and comes in myriad shapes and patterns. Traditional decanters, vases,

A shop window in the Old Town sparkles with Bohemian glass

bowls and glasses, with patterns cut by hand, make pretty souvenirs or gifts and are to be had at roughly half the price of that in other European countries.

More modern designs in **glasswear** are also popular, from large, decorative sculptures to vases. Bunches of large glass flowers mimic the shape of fresh blooms.

The delicate features of Bohemian **porcelain** figurines have changed little in the past 200 years, and their flowing forms are highly prized among collectors. The best originate from small factories around Karlovy Vary, but they can also be bought in Prague. The Český Porcelán factory on the outskirts of town – which also has an outlet on site – is famous for its dinner services in its signature cobalt blue 'onion' design.

With so much beautiful architecture all around you, it is hardly surprising that Prague is a **city of the arts**. Many visitors enjoy having their portrait drawn or painted by the artists on Charles Bridge. There are also numerous stalls selling watercolours or line drawings of Prague. Moody black-and-white photographs offer yet another perspective

The antiques shops of Prague occupy historic premises

of the city. Apart from these more obvious offerings, Prague also has several galleries selling 'serious' art by both established and up-and-coming artists.

Many **antiques dealers** have carved a niche for themselves here, with musical instruments being particularly prevalent. As a leading city of the Hapsburg Empire, Prague counted a large number of wealthy and cosmopolitan citizens who owned treasures from around the world. These collections, along with a rich legacy of Bohemian furniture and artefacts, form the basis of today's trade in antiques.

Garnets have been mined and polished in the Czech Republic for centuries, and the pretty, semiprecious stones can be bought in jewellers across the city. They are often set in gold and silver to create necklaces, bracelets or rings. **Amber** is also popular but much of it is imported from Russia; watch out for fake amber – if you want to buy, go to a reputable dealer.

Shops selling **Czech handicrafts** are often enticingly set in historic houses or converted cellars. Wooden **toys** make good presents for young children: sets of old-fashioned building blocks sit alongside animals mounted on wheels, or assorted farm vehicles. **Ceramics** come in a variety of shapes and sizes, decorated with glazes of almost every hue.

Particularly attractive are the natural shades achieved by the use of earth pigments. Have fun re-creating the city's streets with ceramic miniatures of Prague's historic buildings. Textiles are also good value, with woollen blankets and throws in a range of sizes. In the Czech Republic, **decorated eggs** feature prominently in Easter celebrations and are widely available as souvenirs – coloured ribbons are attached so that you can hang them in your home. A batik process is used to apply wax in a pattern before layering on the colour, which adheres only to the wax-free parts of the egg's surface. The result is a pattern of extraordinary complexity, all the more amazing for its fragile medium. **Marionettes** make an original souvenir and come in a range of characters. The craft stalls of Josefov are appropriately laden with Rabbis; in other parts of the city you will find showbusiness celebrities or cartoon characters. Finally, **basketwear**, still integral to rural living, makes an appearance – although unfortunately the most beautiful items are often the largest and far too bulky for the return flight home.

In a city that inspired Mozart and Beethoven, and where performances of classical **music** will probably feature prominently during your stay, it comes as no surprise that music is readily available, with some stores selling a huge range of classical recordings. Every composer imaginable is covered, with the haunting melodies of Czech composers such as Smetana and Dvořák taking their inspiration from the countryside around Prague.

Decorated Easter eggs make colourful presents

Street musicians often have CDs of their performances for sale

CDs are inexpensive and even the street performers that you encounter often sell CDs of their performance.

Bottles of the Czech pilsner **beer** are rather heavy to take home, but try a bottle of the heady Becherovka liqueur. Plum brandy or *slivovice* is also widely available, as are brandies distilled from other fruits.

SPORTS

Although Prague itself does not cater particularly well to the sports enthusiast, the surrounding Bohemian countryside is beginning to offer pursuits such as kayaking and horseriding.

Spectator sports: **Sparta Praha** is the Czech Republic's top football team and has been one of the leading European clubs for many years. They play in a stadium (tel: 220 570 323) adjacent to Letná Park and their season runs from September to April. **Ice hockey** is extremely popular, the main venue being HC Slavia's Saska Arena stadium (tel: 266 121 122). **Horseracing** takes place every Sunday from April to October at Velká Chuchle, Prague 5 (tel: 257 941 431), with trotting in Spring and Autumn. The Czechs are naturally proud of the number of professional **tennis** players they have produced in recent decades. The National Tennis facility (tel: 224 817 802) on Štvanice Island below the Hlávkův Bridge hosts Grand Prix tournaments. Contact the information office for details.

Participation sports: for a round of **golf**, try the Golf Club Prague (tel: 257 216 584) on the outskirts of the city, or the Exhibition Ground. Alternatively, head out to Karlštejn (tel: 311 604 991), only 28km (16 miles) away, where you can see the course from the castle turrets. Large golf courses are on hand at the spa towns situated a couple of hours away from Prague. The course at Mariánské Lázně (tel: 354 624 300) regularly hosts PGA tournaments, while Karlovy Vary (tel: 353 331 001) features the oldest club in the Czech Republic, inaugurated in 1904.

CHILDREN

At first glance Prague seems to have little to offer children, the accent of a typical tour being on visiting the major churches, palaces and galleries. However, there are a few fun activities that will keep children happy and maybe even amuse parents!

Transport can be entertaining. Ride in a horse-drawn carriage through the streets of the Old Town, or perhaps opt for an open-top vintage car. Boat trips on the Vltava are also fun; take some bread to feed the ducks and swans. A simple ride on a tram can be a great experience in itself, and taking the funicular railway up to Petřín Hill (same ticket) is thrilling for children.

With a little advance planning, a well-chosen **theatre trip** can be a stimulating experience even for small children. The Lanterna Magika features dance, mime and the use of lighting effects. It requires no language skills and concentrates on visual entertainment, ideal for the very young. The National Marionette Theatre (tel: 224 819 322) stages shows for all ages, including a puppet version of *Don Giovanni*.

If your child is mad about **funfairs**, a large one comes to the Prague Exhibition Ground during the summer months.

Child-friendly **museums** include the National Technical Museum, with its displays of vintage vehicles, a reconstructed coal-mine and a noise 'laboratory' where children can have fun producing sounds with different instruments. This is one place where they can be as loud as they want to be.

A horse-drawn carriage rides across Petřín Hill

Or try the National Museum with its collections of tropical insects and animal bones – children are always enthralled by giant insects.

The Toy Museum in the eastern part of Prague Castle will appeal with its large selection of toys from ancient Greece to the present day. Time your visit to the castle to coincide with the hourly changing of the guards in the first courtyard – most impressive at noon.

Kids love the **Mirror Maze** on Petřín Hill, although younger children may find it frightening. Bite-sized lunchtime **concerts**, held at venues across town, can be a great way of introducing children to classical music.

Calendar of Events

Prague's cultural calendar is an extremely busy and ever-changing one, and as such impossible to give full details of here. For up-to-date listings and information, the *Prague Post* is the best source. However, as a guide and to help you plan your trip, here are some of the major annual events taking place both in the city and surrounding areas.

1 January Spectacular New Year celebrations across the city.

April Prague Writers' Festival. Annual meeting of some of the best writers in the world.

May Prague International Marathon (dates vary from year to year).

May–June Prague Spring Festival (Pražské jaro). One of the world's best classical-music festivals, with performances by celebrated musicians at major venues throughout the city.

June Smetana National Opera Festival. Prague Fringe Festival: theatre, puppetry, music, art. Rock for People Festival: open-field music concert in Český Brod. Festival of the Five-Petaled Rose: falconry, fire-throwing and target-jousting in Český Krumlov.

June–July Litomýšl: International Opera Festival.

July International Film Festival at Karlovy Vary: originally a forum for films from Eastern Europe, now embracing worldwide productions. Prague Harp Congress: international harp festival.

July–August Prague Verdi Festival. Displays of music and dance in traditional costume. Communities travel from all over Bohemia and Moravia to venues in the city.

August The Chopin Music Festival, held at venues throughout Bohemia.

September Prague Autumn Festival. International music festival.

October Bi-annual Prague Jazz Festival.

October–November Musica Iudaica. International festival of Jewish music held at synagogues and concert halls.

November–May United Colours of Akropolis at Palác Akropolis. Series of concerts around the theme of musical innovation and experimentation.

December Advent and Christmas-time activities such as craft markets, carol concerts and an open-air arts festival.

EATING OUT

Czech food offers the perfect antidote to the rigours of healthy eating and nouvelle cuisine: honest, filling, often delicious dishes, based on the kind of recipes grandmother kept to herself. You will also find that prices are still relatively low, even after increases in the last few years, and it is very easy to eat well for around £7 ($13) per person. Since the Velvet Revolution, Prague has become one of the busiest tourist cities in Europe, and international chefs and restaurateurs have been quick to take advantage of the new opportunities. There is a surprising amount of international cuisine available, from sushi to Indian curries. The following is a guide to the dishes you might expect to find on the menu in a typical Czech restaurant.

Where to Eat

Places to eat, with which Prague is generously endowed, have until recently had to be licensed by the state; but this system is beginning to change as a growing number of new establishments open and international influences find a foothold in the country.

Apart from conventional restaurants *(restaurace)*, which may be exclusive or geared to a regional or foreign cuisine, the following options are worth seeking out:

Vinárny (wine restaurants – on signs you will see the word *Vinárna*) may have the same menus as ordinary restaurants but place a special emphasis on their wine list. The ambience is often intimate, and possibly historic or folkloric as well.

Pivnice or *hospody* (pubs or taverns) specialise in draught beer and a limited selection of traditional meat platters. The mood is likely to be jolly and the service informal.

Prague's restaurants are often located in vaulted cellars

Kavárny (cafés) are essentially for snacks and sweet pastries, although you may find some hot meals on the menu. On signs you will see the word *Kavárna*.

If you are in a rush and in need of a quick bite, there is a wide range of cheap fast-food outlets and self-service bistros in the city centre.

The atmosphere in Prague's eateries is often colourful or romantic, although the standard of service varies. Most waiters will understand a few English phrases, and some will undoubtedly speak very good English; however, learning a few words of Czech will certainly be appreciated. Smoking is extremely widespread in the Czech Republic, and may be difficult to escape, especially in pubs. Terrace cafés and restaurants help to minimise the problem. If a restaurant becomes busy it is normal practice for diners to share a table – many pubs have long communal tables that seat 10 or 12 people.

Be aware of the hidden charges added by some eateries and pubs. A cover charge of around 30 Kč per person may be added to the bill. Some budget cafés charge for condiments, while others leave appetisers on the table without telling you that there is a charge for them. Pubs often send waiters out with trays of short drinks, but any drinks you consume will be added to your bill, although these charges will be minimal.

Breakfast

Breakfast *(snídaně)* is served by hotels from about 6am to 10.30am. Depending on the establishment, it can be a simple affair of bread, butter and jam with tea or coffee, or something

Prague outdoor dining

far more elaborate. In the better hotels, a lavish hot and cold buffet is usually served, but this often counts as an extra and might mean a hefty additional charge. Another option is to eat out at one of the American-style diners.

Lunch and Dinner

On weekdays, most Czechs eat early – generally at around 7pm – then head to bed in preparation for the working day ahead. However, restaurants in Prague stay open until around 10pm or 11pm, and even later at weekends, when locals go out to enjoy themselves.

Most restaurants post a printed menu *(jídelní lístek)*

near the door, giving you at least an idea of their prices. Nowadays, most cheap, medium-priced and first-class restaurants tend to have menus in English and German as well as Czech.

A menu might be divided into the following categories: *studená jídla* (cold dishes), *polévky* (soups), *teplé předkrmy* (warm starters), *ryby* (fish), *drůbež* (poultry), *hotová jídla* (main courses), and *moučníky* (desserts). A growing number of establishments are offering set

Some restaurants are closed in the afternoons

meals at lunchtime and in the evening in addition to à la carte.

Try a starter of Prague ham *(Pražská Šunka)*, a succulent local speciality. It might come served in thin slices, garnished with cucumber and horseradish; with cheese in miniature sandwiches; or folded into horns and stuffed with cream or cream cheese and horseradish.

Soup is a popular choice at both lunch *(oběd)* and dinner *(večeře)*. Either a fairly light bouillon or, as is more likely, a thick, wholesome soup of potatoes, vegetables and perhaps some meat. A spoonful of whipped cream may also be added. One of the heartiest traditional recipes is *bramborová polévka s houbami* (potato soup with mushrooms). This thick soup flavoured with onion, bacon, carrots, cabbage, parsley and spices can constitute a meal in itself.

The hearty Czech cuisine typically centres on well-roasted pork or beef with thick gravy. This is supplemented with poultry, game or fish dishes – owing to the tradition of seasonal hunting in the surrounding countryside. The generally heavy, savoury food goes down best with cold Czech beer, a brew long held in high esteem by gourmets everywhere.

Meat forms the backbone of Czech cuisine. Always thoroughly cooked, it can be roasted or grilled. The succulent *Pražská hovězí pečeně* (Prague roast beef), a joint of beef stuffed with fried diced ham, peas, egg, onion and spices, is one of the most popular dishes. Also look out for *svíčková pečeně na smetaně*, tasty beef in a cream sauce.

Another gourmet favourite is *Šunka po staročesku* (boiled ham the old-fashioned Bohemian way), with a sauce of plums, prunes, walnut kernels and wine. For a taste of the Austro-Hungarian Empire, you should sample some *gulaš* (goulash), a meat stew flavoured with paprika, or *smažený řízek* (Wiener-schnitzel), a delicious breaded veal escalope. Poultry and game are also popular in Prague, and depending on the season you will find duck, goose, boar and venison on the menu.

Although Bohemia produces some excellent wines, the Czech Republic's best vintages tend to come from Moravia, in the country's east, where the gentle slopes enjoy better sunshine. To be sure of buying a good bottle, head for the Czech National Wine Bank (open Mon–Sat 10am–7pm), at Křižovnická 1.

As an accompaniment, pride of place goes to the dumpling. Either made from bread (*houskové knedlíky*, relatively light) or potato (*bramborové knedlíky*, heavier in texture) you will usually find one or two sliced dumplings on your plate. Vegetables have always played a secondary role in traditional cuisine, and when they do appear in soups and stews seem overcooked. You will often see 'stewed vegetables' on menus in English, which forewarns you that they will definitely not be arriving *al dente*. Sauerkraut *(kyselé zelí)* is the most commonly served – red or white cabbage cooked to a melting consistency in animal fat, sugar and a little wine.

Desserts usually figure in the heavyweight category, for example the tasty *jablkový závin* (apple strudel), with a topping of whipped cream. A slightly more delicate variation, *jablka v županu* (apple baked in flaky pastry) uses whole apples stuffed with sugar, cinnamon and raisins. *Švestkové knedlíky* (plum dumplings) are sprinkled with cheese curd and sugar, and then doused in melted butter. A firm favourite is *palačinka*, ice cream or cream and fruit enveloped in a pancake. Finally, *zmrzlina* (ice cream) or *kompot* (stewed fruit) – sometimes laced with fruit brandy – are old stand-bys.

Prague's Havelská Market is crammed with fresh produce

Vegetarian Cooking

The presence of a large expatriate community has led to the emergence of several vegetarian cafés and restaurants over the past few years. Consequently, many non-vegetarian restaurants now offer a range of options *bez masa* (without meat).

One of the best places for vegetarian food is Albio (Truhlářská 20, tel: 222 325 414, open Mon–Fri 10am–10pm, Sat 1–10pm) near náměstí Republiky, which serves up excellent organic fare in smoke-free surroundings. It has a play area for children, too.

Snacks

Prague is an ideal place for inexpensive snacks or lunch on the move, bought from one of the city's street stands. A *bramborák* is a savoury potato pancake served on a square of paper, delicious despite the greasy fingers. *Pečená klobása* (roasted sausage) rates a paper plate, a slice of rye bread and a squirt of mild mustard – but no fork or knife. They also come hot-dog-style with onions and mustard. *Smažený sýr* is a kind of vegetarian Wienerschnitzel consisting of a slice of fried cheese. *Chlebíčky,* or open sandwiches with a variety of toppings, are also popular in snack bars. You may be offered them if you are invited to a Czech home.

American-style fast-food outlets are plentiful, particularly around Wenceslas Square, and more popular with young Czechs than the traditional snack outlets. Gorgeous ice cream is sold everywhere.

The Art of Drinking

Beer halls are a veritable institution in Bohemia, so much so that some unwritten rules of conduct have evolved over the centuries. This special brand of etiquette dictates that if a man and a woman arrive at a pub together, the man should always enter before the woman in case there is any brawling going on inside. Never bother the waiter, and ask for his assistance before moving any of the chairs. Place a beer mat on the table to indicate that you are ready to order. Don't tip too much (a few crowns will do) or you'll be seen as arrogant. Always raise your glass to your neighbours before drinking and look them square in the eye. And finally, never complain that your beer has too much of a head – it's the local custom.

Drinks

Prague offers a wonderful selection of places to drink, of which a large number also serve light meals, and its architectural wealth ensures a range of superb settings. In addition to this, the city has recently started to witness the re-emergence of the thriving café society of the early 20th century.

Czech beer *(pivo)* has a reputation to be envied, and the intense brewing activity around the city of Plzeň has given the world the *pilsner* style of lager, imitated by many other countries. Naturally, local people are adamant that no other beer tastes quite the same be-

An evening at the U Fleků beer hall comes with live music

cause Plzeň beer gets its distinctive flavour from the alkaline water and the excellence of its hops, a key ingredient, which grow on vast wood-and-wire frames in the Bohemian countryside. The most famous beers are *Pilsener Urquell* from Plzeň (Pilsen), *Budvar* from České Budějovice (Budweis) and *Zlatý Bazant* (Golden Pheasant).

Other well-regarded breweries abound in Prague and the smaller surrounding towns. Several pubs brew their own light *(světle)* or dark *(tmave)* blends, including U Fleků which has been in operation since 1499. All Czech beer is tasty and refreshing but it might be wise to bear in mind that it is probably stronger than what you are used to drinking at home.

Czech **wine** *(víno)* is virtually unknown abroad, so it's likely that you will discover something new and pleasing without having to search very hard. Bohemia produces only a small proportion of the country's total wine output: most of it comes from Moravia, where the hot weather produces sweeter grapes. White is *bílé* and red is *červené*.

A drink local to Karlovy Vary, *becherovka* is made of herbs and served chilled as an aperitif, as is the powerful, sweetish *stará myslivecká*. After-dinner drinks generally take the form of fruit brandies (or schnapps), especially *slivovice* which is made from plums.

Non-alcoholic drinks include pure mineral water, bottled at the spa towns of Karlovy Vary and Mariánské Lázné, fruit juices and international brands of soft drinks. Turkish coffee and Italian-style espresso are also very popular.

Colourful traditional beer tankards on display in a Prague shop window

To Help You Order...

May I see the menu?	**Mohu vidět jídelní listek?**
Can I have it without...?	**Mohu mít bez...?**
I am a vegetarian.	**Jsem vegeterián(ka).** (m/f)
The bill, please.	**Zaplatím.**
I'd like...	**Prosím...**

beer	**pivo**	meat	**maso**
bread	**chleba**	the menu	**jídelní lístek**
butter	**máslo**	milk	**mléko**
cheese	**sýr**	mineral water	**minerálka**
coffee	**kávu**	salad	**salát**
dessert	**moučník**	sugar	**cukr**
egg	**vejce**	tea	**čaj**
ice cream	**zmrzlina**	wine	**víno**

...and Read the Menu

bažant	pheasant	**knedlíky**	dumplings
brambory	potatoes	**králík**	rabbit
drůbež	poultry	**kuře**	chicken
fazole	beans	**květák**	cauliflower
houby	mushrooms	**kyselé zelí**	sauerkraut
hovězí	beef	**ledvinky**	kidneys
hrášek	peas	**pstruh**	trout
hrozny	grapes	**rajská jablka**	tomatoes
hrušky	pears	**rýže**	rice
husa	goose	**špenát**	spinach
jablka	apples	**šrnčí**	venison
jahody	strawberries	**štika**	pike
játra	liver	**šunka**	ham
jazyk	tongue	**švestky**	plums
jehněčí	lamb	**telecí**	veal
kachna	duck	**telecí brzlík**	sweetbreads
kapr	carp	**vepřové**	pork
klobása	sausage	**zajíc**	hare

HANDY TRAVEL TIPS

An A–Z Summary of Practical Information

A

ACCOMMODATION

Hotels. Hotels in Prague are expensive in relation to the other costs of your trip. There are many large hotels and very few of the old-world, family-run establishments that can be found in other cities. Most hotels dating from the communist era have very dour exteriors, although a programme of renovation during the 1990s totally updated many of them, bringing the facilities and interior decoration up to international standards. A few gems from the city's glorious Art Nouveau era have also been refurbished. Most hotels will now have en-suite facilities in all rooms. Access for disabled visitors varies, so address hotels directly with any enquiries if this is a requirement for you.

Prague becomes very crowded with visitors from June to September and around Christmas, so booking ahead is essential to guarantee the standard of accommodation that you want.

Hotel prices generally refer to the cost of a room per night and often appear in euros. Breakfast in smaller, cheaper hotels is included in the room price, but may be extra at four- and five-star hotels. A 22 percent tax may be added along with a municipal tax – always ask whether the room rate includes tax before you make a firm booking.

If you arrive in the city without accommodation, contact the Prague Information Service (tel: 12 444) or Around Prague (tel: 224 491 764). The main train stations have information bureaux that can help you find a place to stay. Some of them will require a deposit which can be non-refundable, so check before you make a reservation.

B&Bs. The number of private homes offering bed-and-breakfast accommodation has grown dramatically in recent years, but prices and facilities differ greatly between establishments. Both Around Prague and Prague Information Service (PIS) offices will be able to assist you *(see Tourist Information, page 128)*. Always check the exact location and transport connections for your accommodation, in addition to the facilities, before you make a firm booking.

I'd like a single room/ double room.	**Chtěl bych jednolůžkový pokoj/dvoulůžkový pokoj.**
with bath/with shower	**s koupelnou/se sprchou**
What's the rate per day?	**Kolik stojí za den?**

AIRPORT

Prague-Ruzyné is situated 20km (13 miles) to the northwest of the city. It has become increasingly busy as the number of people visiting the city shot up during the 1990s. Constantly being updated, it has all the facilities expected of a major international airport. Several of the main international airlines fly there in addition to Czech Airlines (ČSA), including British Airways, Air Canada, KLM and Lufthansa. Most major American airlines fly to Western Europe for onward connections to Prague. ČSA flies nonstop from New York to Prague.

A shuttle bus service operated by CEDAZ (tel: 220 114 286) runs between the airport and náměstí Republiky every 30 minutes from 5.30am–9.30pm. The journey takes about 30 minutes, costing a nominal sum (90 Kč). For an extra fee they will drop you at your hotel.

A cheaper but lengthier option is the No. 119 bus, which travels to the Dejvická metro station from where you can reach the city centre. Buy tickets in the terminal or from the machine at the bus stop.

Where do I get the bus to the city centre/airport?	**Odkud jede autobus do centra města?/na letiště?**
Take these bags to the bus/taxi, please.	**Prosím, odneste tato zavazadla k autobusu/taxi.**

Ask at the airport information desk about taxi fares, currently around 400 Kč. The best way to avoid being overcharged is to call one of these two reputable companies (both with English-speaking staff): AAA Taxi (tel: 140 14) or Profi Taxi (tel: 261 314 151). If you hail a taxi, always agree on a price with the driver before getting in and be aware that he will probably demand more than the ride is worth.

B

BUDGETING FOR YOUR TRIP

Once you have paid for travel and accommodation, living expenses in Prague represent exceptional value despite recent price rises.

Travel to Prague. Scheduled flights from London–Prague can be as cheap as £6 plus taxes thanks to easyJet and other Europe-based budget airlines. Scheduled airfares from the US are advertised at around $700, although deals are available. Eurolines offers a 60-day coach pass at £239–99, or 30 days at £189–259.

Airport transfer. Public transport 12 Kč/taxi fare 400 Kč.

Public-transport tickets. Individual ticket 12 Kč for 20 minutes of travel or five metro stops with no transfer. 20 Kč for 75 minutes of travel with transfer. Day pass 80 Kč. Three-day pass 220 Kč.

Taxis. Prices should be 30 Kč then 22 Kč per kilometre, with an additional charge of 4 Kč per minute for waiting. To avoid overcharging, book a taxi by phone (see AIRPORTS for telephone numbers).

Car hire. Rental for a medium-sized car 2,000–3,500 Kč per day with unlimited mileage.

Hotel. Mid-range hotel per room per night 4,000 Kč–5,000 Kč.

Meals and drinks. Large glass of beer 25–40 Kč (or as much as 90 Kč in touristy establishments such as those on Old Town Square); three-course dinner per person 300–500 Kč; soft drink 30 Kč.

Entertainment. Theatre tickets 400–1,000 Kč with state company, or international performances from around 1,200 Kč. Concert tickets are 100–500 Kč.

Tours. City walking tour (3 hours) 350 Kč; coach tour to Karlštejn Castle (5 hours) 1,000 Kč; Vltava river cruise (2½ hours) 800 Kč.

C

CAMPING

The large camp site on the banks of the Vltava, near the Troja Palace and the zoo, is the closest to the town centre. It has space for caravans and tents with good, if not luxurious, facilities (Autocamp Trojská, Trojská 157, Prague 7; tel: 283 850 487; open all year). The Prague Information Service has details of camp sites in the surrounding area.

CAR HIRE

If you plan to stay in the city rather than touring the countryside, a car may be less of a help than a hindrance. The city is compact, with many streets pedestrianised, and has a cheap and efficient public-transport system. If you do want to hire a vehicle, most of the major international firms operate in the Czech Republic. You can pick up your car at the airport or have it delivered to your hotel.

Prices are not particularly high by international standards, although pricing structures can be complicated. Be clear about what is included in the price and what will be added on. Extras can include local tax (currently 5 percent), additional driver charge, mileage, airport delivery charge and collision-damage waiver. If possible, get an overall final quote from several firms to enable you to compare. It may be cheaper and simpler to book before you arrive.

I'd like to rent a car.	**Chtûl bych si půjčit auto.**
large/small	**velké/malé**
for one day/a week	**na jeden den/týden**
Please include full insurance.	**Prosím, započítejte plné pojištûní.**

The daily hire charge for a medium-sized car (by European standards) is around 2,000–3,500 Kč per day with unlimited mileage. Most companies will have special rates for weekends.

Collision-damage waiver is not compulsory but limits your liability in case of an accident. It adds around 300 Kč per day to the rental cost.

Drivers must be at least 21 years of age and have held a full driving licence for one year.

Avis: at the airport, tel: 235 362 420; in the city at Klimentská 46, Prague 1, tel: 221 851 225, <www.avis.cz>.

A-Rent Car: at the airport, tel: 220 11 43 70; in the city at V Celnici 8 (Millennium Plaza), Prague 1, tel: 224 211 587, <www.arentcar.cz>.

Hertz: at the airport, tel: 233 326 714; in the city at Karlovo náměstí 28, Prague 2, tel: 222 231 010, <www.hertz.cz>.

Europcar: at the airport, tel: 235 364 531; in the city at Pařížská 28, Prague 1, tel: 224 811 290, <www.europcar.cz>.

Sixt: at the airport, tel: 220 115 346; in the city at Pobřežní 1 (Hilton Hotel), Prague 8, tel: 224 842 407, <www.e-sixt.cz>.

CLIMATE

Prague sits in a landlocked country in Central Europe. It tends to experience continental weather patterns springing from Russia, but can experience mild, wet weather from the Atlantic. Winters are on the whole cold and wet, but it can stay dry and clear for long spells. When the wind blows from Russia, it can be extremely cold. Summers are warm but rainy. June and July are two of the rainiest months of the year, while spring and autumn are marked by changeable weather.

		J	F	M	A	M	J	J	A	S	O	N	D
Max.	°F	50	52	64	73	82	88	91	90	84	71	57	50
	°C	10	11	18	23	28	31	33	32	29	22	14	10
Min.	°F	9	10	18	28	36	45	48	46	39	28	23	14
	°C	-13	-12	-8	-2	2	7	9	8	4	-2	-5	-10

CLOTHING

Practical, casual clothing should suit most occasions. In summer, take lightweight clothing but be prepared for showers and bring a warm layer in case it's cool in the evenings. In spring and autumn, a coat or thick jacket is advisable. In winter, take a coat, hat and gloves. For a trip to the opera or ballet, or dinner in a fine restaurant, smart clothing is, however, appropriate.

COMPLAINTS

Any complaints should be addressed initially to the parties responsible. If you are still not happy, contact the Prague Information Service at Na příkopě 20, tel: 12 444, for advice. The Czech retail inspection office (COI, tel. 296 36 62 19; email <info@coi.cz>; <www.coi.cz>) takes action against rogue businesses by sending out inspectors; send them the full details of your experience. They may not be able to help your individual case but will prevent future problems.

CRIME AND SAFETY

Prague is a safe, pleasant city to explore on foot. Violent crime is rare, although petty crime such as car theft and pickpocketing has risen sharply in parallel with the growing number of visitors. It is recommended you take the following precautions:

Leave valuables in the safe at your hotel. Never carry large amounts of cash or flaunt expensive jewellery. Carry valuables in inside pockets and keep bags close to your body. Stay alert on trams and the metro, and in large crowds, for example on Charles Bridge or in Wenceslas Square, where pickpockets might be at work. Do not leave anything behind in vehicles. At night, walk in well-lit streets.

I want to report a theft.	**Chci ohlásit krádež.**
My wallet/handbag/passport/ ticket has been stolen.	**Ukradli mi náprsní tašku peněženku/kabelku/pas/lístek.**

CUSTOMS AND ENTRY REQUIREMENTS

The Czech Republic is in constant consultation with other governments on the topic of customs and entry requirements, which are therefore subject to change. To be certain, check with your nearest consulate. At present the situation is as follows:

Passports/visas. Citizens of the European Union – of which the Czech Republic is now a member – and of most European countries need only a passport to visit the Czech Republic for up to 180 days. Citizens of the United States, Canada, New Zealand and Australia can stay for up to 90 days with a passport. Citizens of South Africa can enter the Czech Republic but must first obtain a visa. All passports must be valid for at least three months from the date of your arrival in the Czech Republic.

Vaccinations. You do not need vaccinations to enter the Czech Republic unless you are travelling from an infected area.

Currency restrictions. There is no restriction on the amount of foreign currency you can import and export. In fact, you must be able to prove, if asked, that you have access to 1,000 Kč per day or 37,000 Kč per month with which to support yourself. In practice, you are unlikely to be asked. As regards the Czech currency, there is an import and export limit of 200,000 Kč. Keep your currency-exchange receipts as you may be required to show them.

Customs. Travellers are allowed to import the following duty-free goods: 200 cigarettes or 100 cigarillos or 50 cigars or 250g of tobacco; 1 litre of spirits; 2 litres of wine; 50ml of perfume or 250ml of eau de Cologne.

You can also import gifts up to a value of 6,000 Kč, as well as all reasonable items for personal use. It is illegal to export antiques without a permit.

D

DRIVING

Road conditions. Road conditions in the Czech Republic are generally good, although signs are not always clear so you will need a good map to get around. Within Prague road conditions are also good, but watch out for cobbled streets and tramlines, both of which become slippery when wet, and confusing one-way systems.

Rules and regulations. Drive on the right and overtake on the left. The speed limits are 130 km/h (80 mph) on motorways, 90 km/h (56 mph) on secondary roads and 60 km/h (37 mph) in built-up areas. Seatbelts are compulsory where fitted, and drink-driving is illegal. Children under the age of 12 are not allowed in the front seat. Drivers are generally patient, but keep a lookout out for trams and pedestrians – many of whom are tourists unfamiliar with the traffic conventions. If you have an accident you must inform the police and wait for them to arrive before moving your vehicle.

Fuel costs. Fuel is cheap by European standards and is priced in litres. Diesel is around 29 Kč and premium unleaded fuel 30 Kč. Service stations are open from 8am–6pm, some till later. Most of the international ones, such as Aral, take credit cards, but independent concerns may not – check before you fill your tank.

Parking. Parking in the city poses some difficulties due to reserved areas and numerous restrictions. A number of private wheel-clamping businesses operate and you will be clamped if you infringe parking regulations. On-street parking is divided into three zones: orange zones are for short-term parking metered at 40 Kč per hour, free parking on Sunday; green zones are for stays of up to 6 hours, metered at 30 Kč per hour, free parking on Sunday; blue zones are for residents or companies in possession of a permit. The main guarded parking area for the city is by the main railway station on Wilsonova, but there are unguarded car parks under Wenceslas Square and near the Hotel Intercontinental in the Jewish Quarter.

If you need help. Dial 1240 to call out the 'yellow angels' or Auto-tourist Road Service (tel: 222 512 053), who will attempt to repair your car or take you to the nearest garage. Call 158 for the police.

Bringing your own car to Prague. You will need a valid driver's licence; vehicle registration/ownership documents; a Green Card extending your insurance; a national identity sticker; a first-aid kit; and a red warning triangle. Drivers must buy a road permit, valid for one year. This can be purchased at the border – current price 1,000 Kč – and must be displayed in the car windscreen. Breakdown insurance is recommended: consult your motoring organisation before you travel.

Jednosměrný provoz	One way
Na silnice se pracuje	Roadworks
Nebezpeči	Danger
Nevstupujte	No entry
Objížďka	Diversion
Opatrně/ Pozor	Caution
Pěší zóna	Pedestrian zone
Snížit rychlost (zpomalit)	Slow down
Vchod	Entrance
Východ	Exit
Full tank, please.	**Plnou nádrž, prosím.**
super/unleaded/diesel	**super/ bezolovnatý/nafta**
I've broken down.	**Mám poruchu.**
There's been an accident.	**Stala se nehoda.**
Can I park here?	**Mohu zde parkovat?**

E

ELECTRICITY

Prague uses the 220V/50 Hz AC current, requiring standard two-pin round continental plugs. Visitors should bring their own adapters.

EMBASSIES/CONSULATES/HIGH COMMISSIONS

UK. Thunovská 14, Prague 1; Tel. 257 402 111.
Ireland. Tržiště 13, Prague 1; Tel. 257 530 061.
US. Tržiště 15, Prague 1; Tel. 257 530 663.
Canada. Muchova 6, Prague 1; Tel. 272 101 800.

EMERGENCIES

Police 158	Fire 150	Paramedics 155

Fire!	Hoří!
Help!	Pomoc!
Stop thief!	Chyt'te zloděje!

G

GAY AND LESBIAN TRAVELLERS

Gay and lesbian travellers will find Prague a welcoming destination. The gay scene is lively, with a number of clubs and bars to enjoy. Try the publication *Radnost (see What to Do)* for listings.

GETTING THERE

By air. Most people travel to the city by air on one of the many daily flights from Europe's major cities. Czech Airlines is the Czech Republic's national carrier <www.csa.cz> and operates direct flights to New York and Newark. However, it also works in partnership with Air France, Delta and Air Canada to reach other North American cities, including Montreal and Toronto. Other Czech Airlines destinations include London and Manchester in the UK, and Dublin in the Republic of Ireland. No US carrier offers direct flights to Prague.

The following airlines fly to Prague from London Heathrow and their own domestic bases: British Airways, Air France (from Paris), KLM (from Amsterdam), Lufthansa (from Frankfurt and other major cities in Germany), Austrian Air (from Vienna), Scandinavian Airlines-SAS (from Stockholm), Malév-Hungarian Airlines (from Budapest) and Alitalia (from Rome). In addition to this, the budget airline easyJet flies from London Gatwick and Stansted, while Jet2, BMI and BMIbaby fly from several other UK airports.

Connections from the US to Europe are possible with American Airlines, Delta Airlines, Continental Airlines, United Airlines and Northwest Airlines. From Australia and New Zealand, travellers can reach Europe for onward flights to Prague through Singapore Airlines, Thai Airways International, Qantas and Air New Zealand.

By rail. Prices for rail travel are sometimes more expensive than air travel and journeys may take longer than by car or plane – for example a 10-hour train ride from Frankfurt which would normally be a mere five-hour drive. Purchasing a rail pass for a set amount of days can help minimise costs. Information be obtained from the main railway station in Prague, tel: 221 111 122 or at <www.vlak.cz>.

By road. *(See also page 116)* Eurolines operates buses that connect the major cities of Europe, <www.eurolines.com>.

GUIDES AND TOURS

A number of tours are available in Prague and into the surrounding countryside. These include walking tours (individual and group), theme tours (perhaps musical or literary), horse-drawn carriage tours, little trains and vintage-car tours, lasting anything from 30 minutes to a whole day. Registered English-speaking guides can be hired by the hour by individuals or groups. Contact Around Prague or Prague Information Service for more information *(see page 128)*.

H

HEALTH AND MEDICAL CARE

Visiting the Czech Republic poses no major health concerns. However, foreign visitors must pay for all medical treatment except emergency treatment, so make sure you have adequate health and accident insurance. It is a good idea to have funds to spare on your credit card or to carry enough extra travellers' cheques to cover minor problems, as you may have to pay in cash and reclaim the cost on your return home.

A number of medical facilities with English-speaking medical personnel cater specifically to visitors. For minor health problems Prague has modern pharmacies (look for a green cross, or the word *lékárna* on the front of the shop), including 24-hour facilities at Štefánikova 6 and Palackého 5. Though the range of drugs available is not as wide as in Western Europe or the US, you will still be able to find remedies for most of the ailments affecting travellers.

The **Diplomatic Health Centre** for foreigners (Na Homolce) is located at Roentgenova 2, Prague 5, tel: 257 272 146.

The **American Medical Centre** can be found at Janovského 48, Prague 7, tel: 220 807 756.

For first aid visit **Health Centre Prague** at Vodičkova 28, Prague 2, tel: 224 220 040.

HITCHHIKING

Although hitchhiking is not illegal in the Czech Republic, it is an inherently dangerous form of travel. Women travelling alone should take extra care, especially as a small number of prostitutes operate on the main highways leading into Western Europe, and drivers may misinterpret the intentions of single female hitchhikers.

L

LANGUAGE

The national language is Czech. However, English is widely spoken, as is German. If you can learn and use a few Czech words, it will always be appreciated.

The Czech alphabet has 33 letters; for instance, c and č are counted as two different letters. Here are a few tips on the pronunciation of the more difficult sounds:

ch like English h	ě like ye in yes	ň like the n in Canute
ř like rs in Persian	j like y in yellow	š like the sh in shine
č like ch in church	c like ts in tsetse	ž like the s in pleasure

M

MAPS

Free maps are available from Around Prague, the Prague Information Service *(see page 128)* and some hotels. Alternatively, Bema Praha's excellent map of Prague can be purchased from many shops.

Do you speak English?	**Mluvíte anglicky?**
I don't speak Czech.	**Nemluvím česky.**
Good morning/Good afternoon	**Dobré jitro/Dobré odpoledne**
Good evening/Good night	**Dobrý večer/Dobrou noc**
Please/Thank you	**Prosím/Děkuji Vám**
That's all right/You're welcome.	**To je v pořádku.**

MEDIA

TV. Most major hotels have cable or satellite TV in each room, with one or more English-speaking news channels. The main ones are CNN, BBC 24 and Sky News. Foreign broadcasts on Czech TV are dubbed rather than subtitled, although there may be English-speaking programmes on other foreign-service TV stations.

Radio. Radio Praha broadcasts news in English three times each day on 101.1 FM; <www.radio.cz>.

Press. All the main foreign-language newspapers are available at news-stands in the city. There are also several English publications printed locally and aimed at visitors to the city. The *Prague Post*, published weekly, contains news and comment as well as events listings. An invaluable resource is *Prague in Your Pocket*, a bi-monthly publication highlighting cultural events around the city. It also includes information on shopping, hotels, cultural festivals and more.

MONEY

The currency of the Czech Republic is the crown or *koruna* (Kč). Each crown is made up of 100 hellers (hal.). There are 5,000 Kč, 2,000 Kč, 1,000 Kč, 500 Kč, 200 Kč, 100 Kč, 50 Kč and 20 Kč notes; and coins of 50 Kč, 20 Kč, 10 Kč, 5 Kč, 2 Kč, 1 Kč and 50 hellers.

Currency Exchange. There are many banks and bureaux de change in the city. Banks open from 8am–4pm, but many close their exchange facilities at lunch time. They charge a standard one percent commission. Bureaux de change have much more flexible hours, often open until 10pm, but can charge up to 30 percent commission – so it pays to shop around. Hotels also change currency but their commission rates vary.

If you want to exchange your remaining crowns back to your own currency before you leave the Czech Republic, you must have an official receipt for your original currency exchange. Beware of black market currency traders. It is illegal to exchange currency in this fashion, and it is often a way of introducing counterfeit notes into the system.

Credit Cards. Credit cards are increasingly accepted for payment across the city. They are now accepted by most hotels, but it is still wise to double-check before paying in a restaurant or a shop.

ATMs. There is a large number of cashpoints that will issue cash against your current-account card or credit card.

Travellers Cheques. These offer a safe way of carrying cash and can be exchanged at banks, but stick to the major issuers. Note that they will not be accepted as payment in shops, restaurants or hotels.

O

OPENING HOURS

Banks are open 8am–4pm (some close from noon–1pm) Monday to Friday. Bureaux de change operate daily, often until 10pm or later.

Some general shops open as early as 6am, while department stores open at 8.30am; both close at around 6pm, although a growing number stay open till 8pm on Thursday. Shops in the centre, particularly those aimed at tourists, often remain open until late in summer.

Museums usually open 10am–6pm and close on Sunday or Monday; exceptions include the Jewish Museum's synagogues (closed Saturday). Most galleries open 10am–6pm but close on Monday.

P

POLICE

There are several types of law enforcement operating in the city. **State police** are responsible for day-to-day policing. They wear white shirts and dark-grey trousers or skirts. They are armed. **Municipal police** wear light-grey trousers or skirts. **Traffic police** are responsible for all road and traffic regulations. They may erect roadblocks to check documents (always carry your driver's licence and passport as well as your car documents) or to breathalyse drivers. This police force also controls fines for parking and clamping infringements. If you are involved in a traffic accident you must inform the police before moving your vehicle *(see page 116)*.

POST OFFICES

Postal services are cheap and reliable for letters and postcards. Most shops that sell postcards also sell stamps, as do many hotels. Public postboxes are either orange with a side slit (old style) or orange-and-blue with a front flap (new style).

The main post office (open 24 hours a day) is at Jindříšská 14, just off Wenceslas Square. Here you can send telegrams, make international calls, and buy stamps and phonecards. Postal rates at the time of printing were: Europe from 9 Kč, further afield from 12 Kč.

PUBLIC HOLIDAYS

Government offices and banks close for the following holidays:

1 January	*Nový rok*	New Year's Day
1 May	*Svátek práce*	May Day
8 May	*Vítězví nad fašismem*	Victory over fascism
5 July	*Slovanští věrozvěsti sv. Cyril a Metoděj*	Slavic Missionaries St Cyril and St Methodius
6 July	*Výročí úmrtí Jana Husa*	Jan Hus's death
28 October	*První československá republika*	First Czechoslovak Republic
24 December	*Štědrý den*	Christmas Eve
25/26 December	*Svátek vánoční*	Christmas/Boxing Day
Movable date	*Velikonoční pondělí*	Easter Monday

PUBLIC TRANSPORT

Prague has a comprehensive and integrated public-transport system that provides a cheap and efficient service. Tickets and passes can be used on all forms of transport.

Each ticket has a time limit and you pay more for a longer limit. The cheapest ticket costs 12 Kč and allows either 20 minutes of travel with no transfer or five stops on the metro with no line change. A 20 Kč ticket allows 75 minutes of travel and allows line change or tram transfer within that time. Children aged 6–15 pay half price.

Tickets can be bought at metro stations (there are automatic ticket machines which give instructions in English and supply change) or newsstands. They must be validated in the small yellow machines you will see when you catch the tram or arrive at the metro.

Day tickets or longer passes are also available and are valid for unlimited travel on all forms of transport. These can often be supplied by your hotel concierge but can also be purchased at the M.H.D. kiosks at all major metro stations. They will be valid from the date stamped on them and do not have to be validated for each journey. Prices are as follows: 24-hour pass 80 Kč; 3-day pass 220 Kč; 7-day pass 280 Kč; 15-day pass 320 Kč.

Trams. There is a comprehensive network of 31 tram routes which connect both sides of the river. Each tram stop shows the tram number passing there and a timetable. Most city maps show the tram routes in addition to the location of the major attractions, and purchasing one of these would be helpful *(see page 121)*. All trams run from 4.30am–midnight, but a number of routes are also designated as night routes and will operate a service 24 hours per day. Purchase your ticket before you travel and validate it as you enter unless you are transferring from another tram or metro within your allotted time.

Metro. The extremely efficient Prague metro opened in 1974 and provides a great service for visitors. There are three interlinked lines, and metro maps can be found at each station. Metro signs above ground feature a stylised M incorporated into an arrow pointing downwards. Metro trains operate until midnight.

Bus. Buses tend to provide a service out to the Prague suburbs rather than compete with trams in the city.

Funicular at Petřín. The ride to the top of Petřín Hill also takes standard tickets. You can buy these at the station before you travel.

Taxis. The most common complaint from visitors to Prague tends to be about taxis; there are some unscrupulous operators out there. Prices are supposed to be about 30 Kč then 22 Kč per kilometre, with an additional charge of 4 Kč per minute for waiting. Phoning a taxi is cheaper than hailing one, as rates are lower and you won't be over-charged. Two reputable firms with staff who speak English are AAA Taxi (tel: 140 14) and Profi Taxi (tel: 261 314 151). If you must hail a taxi, check the rates listed on the passenger door with the meter, or negotiate a price beforehand; a ride in the city centre should not cost more than 100–200 Kč, a trip to the airport should cost about 400 Kč.

R

RELIGION

The Czech Republic is mainly a Catholic country and Prague has a profusion of churches that hold regular services. Some also hold services in English. Times will be posted outside the church, or consult the *Prague Post (see page 122)*. Within the city there is an active Jewish community and there are also Anglican and Baptist churches.

T

TELEPHONES

Note: The telephone system in the Czech Republic has undergone a thorough overhaul, with most phone numbers now consisting of nine digits, including the area code. You should dial the entire nine-digit number even if you are dialling within the same area code. If you do have problems getting through to a number, call the Prague directory enquiries on 1180. They have some English-speaking staff.

Although it is possible to use public phone boxes in the street to make international calls, in practice the service is still in its infancy. You will have more success from a post office (you pay a deposit to start your call and then pay the balance when you have finished) or through your hotel – although they will add on a high surcharge for the service. Some hotels will provide details of international access numbers to organisations such as AT&T. These allow you to make direct international calls at lower rates provided you pay by credit card. The international operator can be contacted on 1181.

Public telephones take phonecards *(telefonní karta)*. These can be bought at post offices or newsstands.

The international code for the Czech Republic is 420. The city code for Prague is 2, but this is included in the nine-digit number so should not be dialled extra.

To call the following countries from Prague dial 00, then the relevant code: **US** 1; **Canada** 1; **United Kingdom** 44; **Ireland** 353.

TICKETS

There is no central ticket office for events in Prague. Visit each individual box office for event tickets, buy from one of the roving ticket sellers in the main square or visit the Prague Information Service (PIS) office in the Old Town Hall *(see page 128)*. Note that prices are often cheaper if you buy tickets direct from the box office.

TIME ZONES

Prague operates on Central European Time (CET). This is one hour ahead of GMT in winter and two hours ahead of GMT in summer.

TIPPING

Tipping is appreciated but levels are low and in some restaurants, service is included in the price – it should state this on the menu.

For other services tips should be as follows:
  Waiter 10 percent
  Taxi driver 10 percent
  Tour guide 60 Kč
  Hotel porter 15 Kč per bag

TOILETS

There are public toilets at each metro station, which should stay open until 9pm. There is usually a small fee of around 2–5 Kč.

If there are no man or woman symbols to help you, ladies' toilets will be labelled *Ženy* or *Dámy,* mens' will be *Muži* or *Páni.*

TOURIST INFORMATION

For information before you leave for Prague contact the Czech Tourist Authority at the following:

UK. Morley House, 320 Regent Street, London W1B 3B6;
tel: (020) 7631 0427, fax: (020) 7631 0419.

US. 1109–11 Madison Avenue, New York, NY 10028;
tel: (212) 288 0830, fax: (212) 288 0971.

Canada. 401 Bay Street, Suite No. 1510, Toronto, Ontario M5H 2Y4;
tel: (01) 416 363 99 28, fax: (01) 416 363 02 39.

The Czech Tourist Authority's information centre in Prague is at Vinohradska 46. There are also many commercial agencies offering tourist information and selling tours. Two reliable organisations are:

Around Prague Tourist Information. Celetná 14, Prague 1, tel: 224 491 764; also in the centre at Karlova 1, Národní 4 and Nerudova 4.
Prague Information Service. Na příkopě 20, Prague 1, tel: 12 444 and in the Old Town Hall, Prague 1, tel: 224 482 562.

W

WEBSITES

The websites for organisations mentioned in this book are included with their contact details, but here are a few websites that may be of help in the research and planning of your trip.

- <www.praguepost.cz> *Prague Post* newspaper
- <www.czechtourism.com> Czech Tourist Authority
- <www.pis.cz> Prague Information Service
- <www.dpp.cz/en> Prague public transport
- <www.pragueiguide.com>
- <www.czech-travel-guide.com>
- <www.inyourpocket.com/cr/prague/en>

Cybercafés. There are a number of web-cafés in Prague, including:
Bohemia Bagel. Masná 2, Prague 1, tel: 224 812 560 and Újezd 16, Prague 1, tel: 257 310 694. Both open daily 7am–midnight.
The Globe Bookstore and Coffeehouse. Pštrossova 6, Prague 1, tel: 224 934 203. Open daily 10am–midnight.
Káva Káva Káva. Národní 37, Prague 1, 224 228 862. Open Mon–Fri 7am–10pm, Sat–Sun 9am–10pm.
Internet Café Spika. Dlážděná 4, Prague 1, tel: 224 211 521. Open daily 8am–midnight.

WEIGHTS AND MEASURES

The Czech Republic uses the metric system.

Y

YOUTH HOSTELS

The Clown & Bard. Bořivojova 102, Prague 3, tel: 222 716 453.
Travellers' Hostel. Dlouhá 33, Prague 1, tel: 224 826 662.
Apple. Králodvorská 16, Prague 1, tel: 222 231 050.

Recommended Hotels

Prague has become one of Europe's most popular tourist destinations, and its number of guest rooms has grown dramatically. There are numerous new hotels along with hotels from the communist era, rather forbidding in appearance despite up-to-date facilities. However, the city does have some hotels in stunning Art Nouveau and historic buildings. Accommodation is relatively expensive and good budget accommodation – such as small, family-owned hotels – is lacking. However, the situation is improving. It is always best to reserve your room before you arrive, especially from June–September and at Christmas time. Rates given below are for the cheapest double room per night in high season and may be listed in euros. Room taxes of 22 percent and a small municipal tax may be extra, so check before booking. Breakfast is not always included and could add 800–1,000 Kč to the room rate. Disabled access is generally better in the more modern hotels.

The following hotel recommendations – price categories indicated in euro symbols – cover all areas of the city, including large and small hotels with local and international management.

If telephoning Prague from outside the Czech Republic dial 00+420 before the numbers listed.

€€€€€	over 6,000 Kč
€€€€	5,000–6,000 Kč
€€€	4,000–5,000 Kč
€€	3,000–4,000 Kč
€	below 3,000 Kč

OLD TOWN AND NEW TOWN

Adria €€ *Václavské náměstí (Wenceslas Square) 26, Prague 1, tel: 221 081 111, fax: 221 081 300, <www.hoteladria.cz>.* This bright, yellow-hued hotel on Wenceslas Square features 88 rooms with polished wood furniture and green-and-gold fixtures. You can book theatre tickets and sightseeing tours at the front desk and exchange currency at the bureau on the hotel's first floor. All rooms here have Internet access, room service and satellite television. Several rooms are available for guests with disabilities.

Apostolic Residence €€ *Staroměstské náměstí 26, Prague 1, tel: 221 632 206, fax: 221 632 558, <www.prague-residence.cz>.* This tiny hotel is in a fantastic location right on the Old Town Square. Rooms have wooden beams and period furniture, along with Internet access, satellite TV and air conditioning. It may be a little on the noisy side – on the square and above a restaurant –but it does have a view of the Astronomical Clock.

Four Seasons €€€€€ *Veleslavínova 2a, Prague 1, tel: 221 427 000, fax: 221 426 977, <www.fourseasons.com/prague>.* Everything you'd expect from the respected hospitality chain, this 161-room hotel on the bank of the Vltava offers stunning views. all rooms have luxury down pillows and duvets, mini-bar, high-speed Internet access and CD players. Spa and fitness centre. Restaurant and bar.

Jalta €€€€€ *Václavské náměstí (Wenceslas Square) 45, Prague 1, tel: 222 822 111, fax: 224 213 866, <www.jalta.cz>.* Despite its monolithic exterior, the 94-room Jalta Hotel consistently scores highly with the choosy business crowd. Rooms are decorated with polished brass and marble, and have satellite television, air-conditioning and mini-bar. Restaurant serves sushi and Asian fusion dishes.

Museum Pension €–€€ *Mezibranská 15, Prague 1, tel: 296 325 186, fax: 296 325 188, <www.pension-museum.cz>.* A fantastic bed and breakfast in a very central location next to the National Museum. Rooms are very large and all face a quiet garden courtyard. Excellent value for money, and perfect for families. Great buffet breakfasts.

Palace Praha €€€€€ *Panská 12, Prague 1, tel: 224 093 111, fax: 224 221 240, <www.palacehotel.cz>.* Just a quick walk from

Wenceslas Square, the Palace is arguably one of the most luxurious and elegant hotels in the city. With its extravagant Art Nouveau decor, 124 rooms done in muted greens and blues, and bathrooms lined with Carrara marble, each room provides a long list of amenities to impress the discerning traveller: air-conditioning, mini-bar, hair dryer and Internet connections. Access for disabled guests. Parking at extra charge.

Paris €€€ *U Obecního domu 1, Prague 1, tel: 222 195 195, fax: 224 225 475, <www.hotel-paris.cz>*. The Hotel Paris, situated next to the Municipal House, was one of Prague's finest establishments when it was built in 1904. Today it has been totally refurbished and is once again at its dazzling best. If you don't stay here, visit the Café de Paris for a drink. Rooms have air-conditioning, TV, phone point, safe, mini-bar, hair dryer, robes. Facilities include gourmet restaurant, bar/café, fitness room/spa, 24-hour room service. 94 rooms.

Radisson SAS Alcron €€€ *Štěpánská 40, Prague 1, tel: 222 820 000, fax: 222 820 100, <www.radissonsas.com>*. In 1999 the Radisson underwent a massive overhaul, making it one of the most sought-after places to stay in Prague. An award-winning Art Deco interior based on an early 20th-century jazz theme, along with two critically acclaimed restaurants, make this hotel hugely popular with travellers from diplomats to CEOs. Facilities include 24-hour room service, a cigar shop, two superior restaurants (the Alcron and La Rotonde), a live jazz bar serving outstanding cocktails and a fitness room with sauna and solarium. Room amenities include Internet access, entertainment system with video games, hair dryer and mini-bar. 211 rooms.

Ungelt €€ *Malá Štupartská 1, Prague 1, tel: 224 828 686, fax: 224 828 181, <www.ungelt.cz>*. An intimate, centrally located hotel with 10 rooms decorated with polished wood, gauzy drapes and crystal chandeliers. The building was once part of a medieval warehouse. Parking available. Room amenities include satellite television, mini-bar and radio. Some of the rooms also have their own kitchenettes.

CASTLE DISTRICT AND LESSER QUARTER

Best Western Kampa €€€–€€€€ *Všehrdova 16, Prague 1, tel: 270 090 833, fax: 257 404 333, <www.euroagentur.com>.* Bare wood and clay tiles combined with an abundance of swords and armoury give this 85-room hotel an air of cosy authenticity. Rooms are basic and clean, the rest of the hotel amazing. Parking and restaurant.

Hoffmeister €€€€€ *Pod Broskou 7, Prague 1, tel: 251 017 111, fax: 251 017 120, <www.hoffmeister.cz>.* This family-owned hotel is situated near the foot of the Old Castle steps and is less than five minutes' walk from Malostranská metro station. Each room is individually and well furnished with original art by Adolf Hoffmeister, father of the present owner. Rooms have air-conditioning, TV, phone, mini-bar. Gourmet restaurant, bar and pretty terrace. Parking at an extra charge. 36 rooms.

Savoy €€€€€ *Keplerova 6, Prague 1, tel: 224 302 430, fax: 224 302 128, <www.hotel-savoy.cz>.* An elegant, 59-room hotel overlooking the spires of the castle district. Rooms are decorated in lush red and deep blue, bathrooms in marble and chrome. A relaxation/fitness centre with sauna, whirlpool and steambath is at hand. 24-hour room service, hair salon, office with business and secretarial services.

Sax €€ *Jánský Vršek 3, Prague 1, tel: 257 531 268, fax: 257 534 101, <www.sax.cz>.* This simply-decorated hotel lacks the panache of its neighbours, but a glass-topped atrium and sweeping views of the castle are handsome compensation. Rooms with mini-bar, hair dryer and satellite television. Restaurant. 22 rooms.

U Krále Karla €€–€€€€ *Úvoz 4, Prague 1, tel: 257 531 211, fax: 257 533 591, <www.romantichotels.cz>.* This baroque building (it took its present form in 1639) is in a quiet and convenient location at the top of the hill, looking out over Petřín Hill. The rooms have a distinct Central European kitsch appeal, but many people love the stained-glass windows. Parking and restaurant.

U Tří Pštrosů (At the Three Ostriches) €€€–€€€€ *Dražického náměstí 12, Prague 1, tel: 257 532 410, fax: 257 533 217, <www.upstrosu.cz>.* A Czech classic, this intimate, 18-room courtyard hotel is right next to Charles Bridge and the perfect Lesser Quarter base for exploring the city. The hotel was named after one of its owners, an ostrich-feather salesman. Some rooms contain original Renaissance ceilings and antique desks. Restaurant and bar.

FURTHER AFIELD

Andel's €€€€€ *Stroupežnického 21, Prague 5, tel: 296 889 688, fax: 296 889 999, <www.andelshotel.com>.* All sharp angles, glass and rough stone, Andel's is flanked by a shopping mall, two multiplexes and various eateries. Rooms are designed in minimalist style with glass desks, concealed lighting and DVD players. Restaurant, bar and health club with solarium.

Belvedere €–€€€ *Milady Horákové 19, Prague 7, tel: 220 106 111, fax: 233 372 368, <www.hotelbelvedere.cz>.* Basic and pleasant 155-room hotel near the National Museum of Modern Art. Breakfast served in the hotel's 200-seat ballroom. On-site babysitter. Small pets allowed.

Club Hotel Praha €€–€€€€ *Průhonice 400, tel: 274 010 261, <www.club-hotel-praha.cz>.* A 20-minute drive out of the city just off the D1 ring road, Club Hotel is set on a wooded site with good sporting facilities: tennis courts, squash, badminton and bowling. Rooms have TV, mini-bar, hair dryer. Restaurant, bar, fitness centre, pool, sauna, solarium, parking. Shuttle bus to the city centre. 100 rooms.

Diplomat €€€€€ *Evropská 15, Prague 6, tel: 296 559 111, fax: 296 559 215, <www.diplomatpraha.cz>.* A popular spot with the business crowd, this boxy hotel is a short walk from a metro station, making it convenient for the city centre. Rooms have standard furnishings, but some rooms feature bidets, trouser presses and bathrobes. Parking.

Recommended Restaurants

Food is still very affordable in Prague despite price increases in recent years. If you want to eat at a particular establishment it would be better to make a reservation, particularly at peak periods such as weekends and during the high season. All but the finest restaurants accept casual dress.

Charges may be added to your bill. Some of the more upmarket or tourist-oriented establishments have a small cover charge – it pays to read the menu carefully if you're on a budget – and the Czech 22 percent Value Added Tax (VAT) is usually added. Although credit cards are more widely accepted in Prague restaurants than ever before, this is not universal.

Most restaurants close between lunch and dinner; where food is served without a break this is advertised as 'non-stop'. Lunch is generally between 11am–3pm and dinner 6.30pm–10pm.

The following selection of restaurants includes establishments in all price categories and features a range of cuisine, with many Czech and some international restaurants. Prices are per person and based on a three-course dinner without drinks. If you wish to make a reservation from outside the Czech Republic dial 00+420 before the numbers listed in this guide.

€€€€€	over 1,000 Kč
€€€€	700–1,000 Kč
€€€	500-700 Kč
€€	300-500 Kč
€	under 300 Kč

OLD TOWN AND NEW TOWN

Bellevue €€€€€ *Smetanovo nábřeží 18, tel: 222 221 443, <www. pfd.cz>*. True to its name, Bellevue delivers a remarkable view of the Vltava River and Prague Castle – especially when the two are lit up at night – and serves an outstanding, carefully crafted continental cuisine. Featuring a sublimely elegant decor, its clientele list reads like a who's who of Prague society. Imaginative dishes include Australian veal tenderloin with duck-liver foie gras in truffle sauce, and tempura of tiger prawn with soya caramel. The desserts are equally memorable. Open daily noon–3pm and 5.30pm–11pm. Sun from 11am.

Country Life €–€€ *Melantrichova 15, tel: 224 213 366, <www. countrylife.cz>*. A self-service vegetarian eatery, this is one of the few places in the city that also offers vegan dishes. Non-smoking dining room. Open 9am–8.30pm, Fri 9am–4pm, Sun 11am–8.30pm, closed Sat. Cash only.

Ferdinanda € *Corner of Opletalova and Politických vězňů, tel: 222 244 302, <www.ferdinanda.cz>*. A cheap, modern and friendly Czech restaurant with a light industrial theme, just off Wenceslas Square. Try the delicious goulash and sample the Sedm Kulí beer (named after the seven bullets that killed archduke Franz Ferdinand) that is brewed on the premises. Open daily 8am–11pm, Sat and Sun from 11am.

Jáma €–€€ *V jámě 7, tel: 224 222 383, <www.jamapub.cz>*. A popular place of expat legend, this restaurant-cum-bar serves up Mexican and American dishes, which include *fajitas* and giant chilli burgers. American-style breakfasts are available at the weekend, including French toast and pancakes. Open daily 11am–1am.

Klub Architektů € *Betlémské náměstí 5A, tel: 224 401 214.* Situated just opposite the Bethlehem Church and under an architecture bookshop, this restaurant is a little haven of peace. Along with meaty options, there are lots of vegetarian offerings: salads, soups and more exotic dishes, served up in a minimalist, bare-walled cellar (appropriately low-key given the architects above and the Hussite church close by). Friendly staff and low prices add to its allure, as does the no-smoking area. Open daily 11.30am–midnight.

L'Angolo €€€ *Dlouhá 7, Prague 1, tel: 224 829 355.* A new upmarket Italian restaurant and pizzeria located on a street corner just off Old Town Square. It offers the full range of Italian cuisine, with enticing starters and desserts on display upstairs. Reservations recommended.

La Perle de Prague €€€€€ *Tančící dům, Rašínovo nábřeží 80, tel: 221 984 160, <www.laperle.cz>.* Located on the top floor of one of Prague's most famous modern landmarks, Frank Gehry's 'dancing' or 'Fred and Ginger' building – so-called because of its flowing forms – La Perle de Prague offers the diner sweeping views of the city from both the inside dining room and the rooftop terrace. La Perle's French cuisine is among the best in Prague, and the menu changes with the seasons. Open daily for lunch noon–2pm, and for dinner 7pm–10.30pm. Advance reservations recommended.

La Scene €€€€€ *U milosrdných 6, Prague 1, tel: 222 312 677, <www.lascene.cz>.* A fabulous designer restaurant, wine bar and champagne club situated close to the Spanish Synagogue. The Michelin-starred chef serves up delicious French dishes, such as the magret duck with thyme, fennel and coriander. The wine and champagne list is one of the best in Prague, and the waiters are both knowledgeable and courteous. Reservations highly recommended. Open noon–2pm and 7pm–11pm, Sat 7pm–11pm, Sun closed.

La Veranda €€€€ *Elišky Krásnohorské 2, Prague 1, tel: 224 814 733, <www.laveranda.cz>.* A gourmet restaurant near the Spanish Synagogue, La Veranda is a light, stylish venue filled with flowers. It specialises in delicate fish dishes but has good meat and vegetarian options too. Excellent service and above average prices, but certainly worth the splurge. Open Mon–Sat noon–11pm, Sun noon–10pm.

Pivovarský dům € *Lipová 15, Prague 2, tel: 296 216 666.* This microbrewery, with traditional Czech decor and a pub atmosphere, features an extensive menu of hard-to-find Czech specialities including fruit-filled dumplings covered in a soft, creamy cheese. The restaurant's extensive beer list boasts some fairly unorthodox flavours such as coffee and champagne. Open daily 11am–11.30pm.

Rybí Trh €€€–€€€€ *Týn 5, tel: 224 895 447, <www.rybitrh. cz>.* Nestling in the shadow of the Church of Our Lady of Týn, this restaurant serves fish dishes only. Fresh fish, lobster and other varieties of seafood are flown in daily to offer you the widest choice, and then cooked to your precise requirements. An outdoor terrace makes a pretty setting for summer dining. Open daily 11am–midnight.

Taj Mahal €€–€€€ *Škrétova 10, tel: 224 225 566, <www. tajmahal.cz>.* A local institution, this Indian restaurant is just a short distance from the National Museum. Cuisine is as authentic as it comes in Prague, including exotic masalas and vindaloos packed full of flavour. Open Mon–Fri 11.30am–11.30pm, Sat–Sun 1pm–11.30 pm.

U Bílé Krávy €€–€€€ *Rubešova 10, tel: 224 239 570, <www. bilakrava.cz>.* The 'White Cow' owes its name to the occupation of its owner, who doubles as a cattle farmer in Burgundy, France. Most of the dishes use meat from his herd, flown directly into Prague, but a variety of seafood, lamb and rabbit dishes also have their place on the menu. A wood-beamed, cottage-like interior complements an ambitious menu that ranges from *escargots* in red wine to bœuf bourguignon. Open Mon–Fri 11.30am–11pm, Sat and Sun closed.

U Fleků €€ *Křemencova 11, Prague 1, tel: 224 934 019, <www. ufleku.cz>.* Not so much a restaurant as a compulsory part of the Prague experience, this old-style beer hall is usually packed with mug-waving, accordion-playing Czechs, all singing and swaying in unison. The beer prices outstrip what you would normally pay in a local pub, but the atmosphere alone makes it worth every penny. Extremely popular and often crowded. Open daily 9am–11pm.

U Kalicha €–€€ *Na Bojišti 12, tel: 296 189 600, <www.ukalicha. cz>*. 'The Chalice' restaurant and pub, with its old wooden interior, is an affectionate tribute to the author who wrote the classic Czech novel *The Good Soldier Švejk*. The kitchen specialises in authentic Czech cuisine, from classic beef goulash to roasted goose with dumplings. The restaurant's atmosphere is a lively one, with singing and beer-quaffing locals. Open daily 11am–11pm. Reservations essential.

U Modré Růže €€€€ *Rytířská 16, tel: 224 225 873, <www. umodreruze.cz>*. 'At The Blue Rose' is an enchanting cellar restaurant with an earthy decor, just a short distance from the Můstek metro station. The kitchen produces fantastic Czech and continental dishes, and those with a taste for wild game will be well-catered for: deer, pheasant and duck all feature on the menu. Open daily 11.30am–11.30pm.

Universal € *V Jirchářích 6, Prague 1, tel: 224 934 416*. One of the best bargains in town serving tasty main courses with a French twist. Meal-sized salads and desserts are as good as you'll find anywhere and at unbelievably reasonable prices. Reservations several days in advance are mandatory at peak hours. Open daily 11.30am–midnight

CASTLE DISTRICT AND LESSER QUARTER

Bakeshop Diner € *Lažeňská 19, tel: 257 534 244*. Freshly baked breads and outstanding handmade sandwiches keep this informal, cafeteria-style restaurant consistently packed. The prices are a little steep compared to standard Czech fare, but the indulgence is worth it. Open daily 7am–10pm.

Café Savoy €–€€€ *Vítězná 5, tel: 257 311 562, <www.cafesavoy. cz>*. Although not strictly a restaurant, this café in the south corner of the Lesser Quarter is one of the most popular places in Prague to stop for refreshment. Choose between excellent gourmet food, the café menu or the home-made cakes underneath a beautifully restored neo-Renaissance ceiling. Open daily 8am–midnight.

David €€€ *Tržiště 21, tel: 257 533 109, <www.restaurant-david.cz>*. Located just a stone's throw from the US Embassy, this bistro prides itself on being a quiet, family-oriented restaurant. The decor is simple – whitewashed walls and white tablecloths – and the cuisine is quintessential Czech with a sprinkling of international dishes, such as New Zealand lamb and baked Norway salmon. Extensive wine list. Open daily 11.30am–11pm.

Gitanes €€ *Tržiště 7, tel: 257 530 163, <www.gitanes.cz>*. A quirky and comfortable Bosnian/Serbian/Montenegran restaurant. Prettily-painted floral ceiling and furnishings, plus a cosy hideaway for two behind a curtain, put you in the right mood. The good Balkan dishes (stuffed peppers, home-made lamb sausage, grilled mushrooms) and an eclectic and interesting wine list mean this place is well worth a visit. Wonderful music makes you feel like you are dining to the soundtrack of a Kusturica movie. Open daily noon–midnight.

Malý Buddha € *Úvoz 44, Prague 1, tel: 220 513 894*. A serene tea-house atmosphere is the setting for fresh and delicious Asian cuisine, such as spring rolls and glass noodles with vegetables, along with an impressive selection of exotic juices. Open Tues–Sun 1–10.30pm. Cash only.

Pálffy Palác €€€€–€€€€€ *Valdštejnská 14, Prague 1, tel: 257 530 522, <www.palffy.cz>*. In operation since the 17th century, this elegant, Baroque restaurant has catered for everyone from diplomats to politicians in its time. An outdoor terrace leads out to breathtaking views of the castle and surrounding gardens. The restaurant's continental/French menu features duck breast with preserved oranges and grilled tiger prawns. Open daily 11am–11pm.

Square €€ *Malostranské náměstí 5, Prague 1, tel: 257 532 109, <www.squarerestaurant.cz>*. A truly international menu includes paella, roast rack of lamb and orange tiramisu. The food is outstanding and the presentation is even better: most dishes look like installations from an art gallery. A good place for breakfast before heading up the hill to the castle. Open daily 8am–1pm.

U Malířů €€€€€ *Maltézské náměstí 11, tel: 257 530 000, <www. umaliru.cz>*. This restaurant is said to be the most expensive in Prague – although by international standards it still offers value for money. It is found on a quiet square in the Lesser Quarter. French *haute cuisine* is served in a beautiful 15th-century dining room complete with an elaborately decorated ceiling, and a tiny outdoor terrace completes the picture. Absolutely perfect for that special occasion. Open 11.30am–midnight.

U Modré Kachnicky €–€€€ *Nebovidská 6, tel: 257 320 308, <www.umodrekachnicky.cz>*. 'At the Blue Duckling' is a popular restaurant near Maltézské náměstí, which features Art Nouveau images on the walls and old-fashioned decor, with lots of dark wood and overstuffed chairs. Traditional Czech cuisine is featured on the menu, as is plenty of game and fish. Open daily 11.30am– midnight.

U Patrona €€€€ *Dražického náměstí 4, Prague 1, tel: 257 530 725, <www.upatrona.cz>*. These little elegant dining rooms are a good place in which to try well-prepared Bohemian specialities. They include a tasty game *consommé* and excellent roast goose with red cabbage. All helped along by some very smooth service. Open daily 10am–midnight.

U Vladaře €€€–€€€€ *Maltézské náměstí 10, tel. 257 534 121, <www.uvladare.cz>*. In business since 1779, this restaurant has several vaulted dining areas as well as an attractive outside terrace. It serves traditional Czech dishes and international cuisine, but it is best known for its mixed grill specialities. Open daily noon–midnight.

U Zlaté Hrušky €€€–€€€€ *Nový svět 3, tel: 220 514 778, <www.zlatahruska.cz>*. On a peaceful street near the castle, 'At the Golden Pear' is one of the most popular cellar eateries in Prague. The dining room is of classic design. Main courses are largely traditional Czech, but steaks, wild game and fish dishes are also featured on the menu. Open daily 11.30am–3pm and 6.30pm–midnight.

INDEX

OTHER BERLITZ TITLES INCLUDE:

Alaska
Algarve
Amsterdam
Athens
Australia
Bahamas
Bali & Lombok
Barcelona
Beijing
Belgium
Berlin
Bermuda
Boston
Bruges & Ghent
Brussels
Budapest
Buenos Aires
Bulgaria
California
Canada
Canary Islands
Cancún & Cozumel
Cape Town
Channel Islands
Chicago
China
Copenhagen
Corfu
Costa Blanca
Costa del Sol
Costa Dorada
  & Tarragona
Crete
Croatia
Cuba
Cyprus
Dominican Rep.
Dublin
Dubrovnik
Edinburgh
Egypt
Florence
Florida
France

French Riviera
Gran Canaria
Grand Canyon
Greece
Greek Islands
Hawaii
Hong Kong
Ibiza & Formentera
Iceland
India
Ireland
Istanbul
Italy
Jamaica
Japan
Kenya
The Lake District
Las Vegas
Libya
Lille
Lisbon
London
Los Angeles
Madeira
Mallorca
Mallorca &
  Menorca
Malaysia
Malta
Mauritius
Menorca
Mexico
Miami
Milan & the
  Italian Lakes
Morocco
Moscow &
  St Petersburg
Munich
Naples
New York
New Zealand
Orlando
Paris

Poland
Portugal
Provence
Puerto Vallarta
  & Acapulco
Qatar
Reykjavík
Rhodes
Riga
Rio de Janeiro
Romania
Rome
Salzburg
San Francisco
Sardinia
Scotland
Singapore
South Africa
Spain
Stockholm
Sweden
Switzerland
Sydney
Tallinn
Tenerife
Thailand
Tokyo
Toronto
Tunisia
Turin
Turkey
Tuscany
USA
Valencia
Vancouver
Venice
Vienna
Vietnam
Vilnius
Virgin Islands
Walt Disney World
  & Orlando
Zákynthos &
  Kefalloniá